Rhetoric as Philosophy

Rhetoric as Philosophy

The Humanist Tradition

Ernesto Grassi

The Pennsylvania State University Press
University Park and London

Acknowledgments

Some of the material of this volume was originally delivered as lectures at Columbia University, The Pennsylvania State University, and Yale University.

Chapter 2 was published in *Philosophy and Rhetoric,* vol. 9, no. 4, 1976. Chapter 4 was first published as a two-part article, "Can Rhetoric Provide a New Basis for Philosophizing? The Humanist Tradition," in *Philosophy and Rhetoric,* vol. 11, nos. 1 and 2, 1978. Chapters 1, 4, and 5 were translated by John Michael Krois. Chapters 2 and 3 were translated by Azizeh Azodi.

I wish to thank Professor Gerard A. Hauser for his editorial assistance.

Library of Congress Cataloging in Publication Data

Grassi, Ernesto.
  Rhetoric as philosophy.

  Includes bibliographical references.
  1. Rhetoric—Philosophy. 2. Philosophy—
History. 3. Humanism—History. I. Title.
PN175.G68   808'.001   79-25276
ISBN 0-271-00256-5

For Donald Phillip Verene

Reflecting thankfulness and a bond which arises from
dedication to a shared concern—the relation of the hidden
humanistic tradition which culminates in the thought of
Giambattista Vico.

You recall Virgil's *Aeneid*, 6, 136f.: Aeneas, commanded
by the Sybil, must obtain a "golden bough" in order to enter
with it into the underworld of the dead. Your "golden bough"
is the *universale fantastico*, the metaphorical image, in whose sign
you were the first to have awakened the dead Vico and so have
today brought the humanist philosophical tradition to speak
again.

Two quotations may here point the way for our further
work together. "Rem vero pro re, quod non est alterius quam
poete, posuit in aureo ramo quem discerpendum Sibilla monuit
antequam [Aeneas] inferos adiret" (Salutati, *De laboribus
Herculis*). "To put one thing in the place of another is possible
for no one but a poet, as [when Virgil presents] the golden
bough that the Sybil called for Aeneas to break off before
entering the underworld."

"On ne se peut ouvrir la région des ombres qu'avec le
rameau d'or, et il faut une jeune main pour le cueillir"
(Chateaubriand, *Mémoires d'outre-tombe*). "One can enter the
realm of the shades only with a golden bough and for this a
young hand is necessary."

Contents

Introduction:
The Roots of the
Italian Humanistic Tradition

It may seem odd that I begin the introduction to the problem of rhetoric with a personal experience. The objection might be raised that this starting point is restricted in time and space and that, accordingly, the investigation that proceeds from this can be directed only to those who have had similar experiences in their lives.

I do not share this view. Every problem that concerns us may not and cannot be conceived in an abstract and purely formal way. If the question that presents itself to us has a basis, then it must bear upon us in a way that oversteps subjective limits. In this introduction and in the following chapters I try to develop a philosophical interpretation of rhetoric. Since philosophy's significance today is usually only recognized in the framework of formal logic, my concern is to investigate whether my comments and suggestions can be shown to have a historical and theoretical background and a principal significance beyond formal logic.

For this reason in this introduction I plan to put the American readers in a position to understand a world that is probably unknown to them, in order to provide them with the perspective necessary for understanding the present investigation. It was the necessity of clarifying my own intellectual identity that forced me to seek and define the significance of the Italian humanistic tradition and rhetoric, a process that took place as the critical confrontation with German Idealism, on the one hand, and the thought of Heidegger—with whom I worked for ten years in Freiburg—on the other.

The Rejection of the Philosophical Importance
of the Latin Tradition

I must call to mind the philosophical situation of Italian philosophy in the 1920s, the time when my studies took place.

At that time Hegelian philosophy predominated in Italy through Croce and Gentile and had been introduced already at the end of the nineteenth century by Bertrando Spaventa. In his work *La filosofia italiana nelle sue relazioni colla filosofia europea,* he indicated explicitly that the thought of the Italian tradition as it was expressed in Renaissance philosophy and in Humanism was partially repressed through the funeral pyres of the Inquisition but then was continued in German idealistic philosophy.[1] In a way that was both polemic and programmatic, he presented the following thesis.

> The philosophical Italian Idea was not extinguished on the funeral pyres of our philosophers but rather grew further in areas that were freer and in minds that were freer. For this reason the search for it in its new father-land, in Germany, is not a servile imitation of German philosophy, but rather the reconquering of something that already had belonged to us. Not our philosophers of the last two hundred years but Spinoza, Kant, Fichte, Schelling, and Hegel are the true students of Bruno, Vanini, Campanella, and Vico.[2]

And Spaventa continues, "The development of German thought is natural, free, and independent, in a word, it is critical. The development of Italian thought is unsteady, hindered, and dogmatic. This is the great difference. . . . Before we again begin to philosophize, we must return to ourselves. . . . Only this way will we create . . . an enduring and historical Italy in the world of thought."[3]

I myself was educated in this spirit and want to mention one episode concerning it. When I came to Freiburg as a young student and visited Husserl, after being checked by Frau Husserl—as was the custom then to see if I was worthy of a meeting with her husband—Husserl said to me at the beginning of our conversation that as an Italian I was predestined to be a philosopher. This comment astonished me in the extreme, and I asked him to explain what he meant by it. Husserl answered me from the presupposition of his phenomenology, "Because the Italians, in contrast to the Germans, are not weighed down by the history of philosophy and therefore can immediately go to the phenomena and their immediate phenomenological investigation." When I explained to him that this was in no way the case, since I was educated in the tradition of Hegelian philosophy, he said to me with genuine dismay, "You poor fellow, then you are lost. Then you no longer have any possibilities left to philosophize." I recall this episode because it is characteristic of the situation at that time.

The influence of German Idealism at that time also affected philosophic attitudes toward the humanistic tradition; in accordance with Hegel's judgments in his *History of Philosophy*,[4] Descartes's work was seen as the beginning of modern thought. What preceded him was considered to be only a more or less confused anticipation of what Descartes's Rationalism then brought to speculative clarity. The attempts of humanistic and Renaissance philosophy at thought were considered to be philosophizing that did not lead to the clarity of conceptual thinking, that is, to be meditation that did not get beyond sensory and imagistic thought. Hence rhetoric, *sensus communis*, and every form of poetic expression were rejected as not belonging to philosophy.

This situation was made more complicated in the 1920s by the predominating political conditions. Gentile—as the ideologian of Fascism—had, from a purely political standpoint, the greatest interest in seeing a new evaluation of Humanism and Renaissance thought as a purely Italian affair. But he was at the same time hindered theoretically to an extent because of his idealistic presuppositions. In this way Humanism and Renaissance philosophy were treated as having primarily historical interest; in general they were considered as the first witnesses of a new evaluation of man, history, and immanent values in contrast to medieval philosophy and the primacy of theology.

In 1928 I decided to leave Italy and to look around Germany, with Scheler, Nicolai Hartmann, and Jaspers, and actually by chance came to Heidegger, who at that time was still unknown. A few of his seminars and lecture courses in Marburg were enough for me to decide to work with him. After he came to Freiburg as Husserl's successor, I worked with him there for ten years. I later broke with him fully because of his behavior in regard to his Jewish friends. This had nothing to do with the intellectual problems that concerned us, despite the fact that it was of principal historical importance for the judgment of Heidegger's moral conduct at that time. I was the first one to write in Italy—in a journal of Gentile's—about Heidegger, and I dedicated my *Habilitation* thesis to him.

Why do I mention this here? Because Heidegger—as incidentally the greatest part of the German tradition—directed his whole effort to rediscovery of Greek thought, a tradition that can be discerned from Hölderlin, Hegel, and Schelling up to him. This included his almost always polemically formulated rejection of Latin thought as something without speculative importance. Cicero seemed to him to be a mere representative of a misunderstood eclecticism of Greek thought. Let us also not forget that Hegel as well maintained that Cicero belonged to "popular philosophy," Cicero not being able to rise from the particular to the general.[5] Carl Prantl denies resolutely in his *Geschichte der Logik* that Cicero's utilization of Greek philosophy has any speculative significance: "In general the passages in which Cicero mentions Aristotle's name arouse indignation." Mommsen, too, speaks of "Cicero's ghastly desolation of thought." The same judgment is found today in the Pauly-Wissowa *Reallexikon*.[6] With Ortega y Gasset, who was sporadically present at Heidegger's lectures from 1929 to 1931, I noticed repeatedly this basic "Germanic" characteristic of Heidegger. Because of this attitude of Heidegger I was forced again and again to reconsider the question of my intellectual identity. When with W. F. Otto and the great classical philologist Karl Reinhardt I edited the *Jahrbücher der geistigen Überlieferung*—which were subsequently forbidden—I was able to outline in the first volume for the first time the problem of the philosophical significance of Humanism in my article "Der Beginn des modernen Denkens."[7] I believe this article contains in essence all that with which I have concerned myself repeatedly in my reflection on Italian Humanism.

Vico's Thought as the Highest Level of Philosophical Consciousness in the Latin Tradition

I began with this autobiographical reference because I believe it is always important to return to the personal situation out of which one's own thought arises, in order to clarify the theoretical problems that concern one's self.

Does the Italian humanistic tradition have a philosophical or only a purely historical significance? If it has a philosophical importance, of what does it consist in our contemporary situation? Finally does this tradition have its origin in the Latin literature, and if so, where primarily?

In order to answer this question I must begin, if only briefly, with a consideration of today's general conception of scientific thought which, especially in the Anglo-Saxon world, is characterized by a certain formalism. Accordingly all "humanistic" thought and all metaphysics must be despised.

That thought is considered to be scientific which proceeds in the framework of a rational process, i.e., in the sphere of proof. This thesis is set forth in modern logical theory in a significant way in Wittgenstein's *Tractatus logico-philosophicus*. [8] Assertion and contradiction are possible only in the context of a system. Outside the symbolic world of the system we have only silence and mystery. The presuppositions upon which the system is based cannot be founded upon the system itself. Hence in its scientific form language is and can be only the expression of objects in "states of affairs," i.e., the only acceptable language is the logical, since it alone puts the rationality in question into words. "The description of the most general propositional form is the description of the one and only general primitive sign in logic." [9] The rejection of all passionate rhetorical language and at the same time all ordinary language as the expression of common sense is based on this. On the other hand this marks the emergence of the ideal of language as a calculus with a mathematical structure that is reduced to the function of formalizing symbols.

Can the Italian humanistic tradition still contribute something effective in opposition to such a view? I know how greatly Anglo-American philosophy is governed by the influence of formal logic, and I cannot claim to be in a position to make any critical commentary on this topic. I only want to present you with my tradition as a beginning point for your own reflection. I believe that I can accomplish my task only if I begin with the thought of that philosopher who in my judgment saw most deeply and most fully the tradition of Italian Humanism in all of its implications. I am referring to Giambattista Vico, to whom the Americans—and not the Europeans—dedicated an international congress in 1976 in New York, which I think is indicative of the intellectual openness of this country.

(a) As we know, Vico takes the object of philosophy to be speculation about history and not nature, and he does this because, as he says, man makes history himself but he does not make nature.

> But in the night of thick darkness enveloping the earliest antiquity, so remote from ourselves, there shines the eternal and never failing light of a truth beyond all question: that the world of civil society has certainly

been made by men, and that its principles are therefore to be found within the modifications of our own human mind. Whoever reflects on this cannot but marvel that the philosophers should have bent all energies to the study of the world of nature . . . and that they should have neglected the study of the world of nations, or civil world, which, since men had made it, men could come to know.[10]

(b) From this results one essential conclusion. The range of Vico's thesis does not consist exclusively or even primarily—as is usually assumed—in the identity of *verum* and *factum,* but rather in the fact that scientific thought is liberated from all formalism. The problems that concern human beings—and these are the only kinds that can have scientific interest—are the ones that urge themselves upon us in the construction of the human world and therefore concern the realization of man as such. Hence we have the primacy of the question of the origin of history.

With this Vico rejects every a priori derivation of metaphysics. From this comes his constant polemic against Descartes and the attempt to derive scientific thought from original, independent, underived principles. Hence the rejection of "critical thinking."

(c) But how and where and in what form do the questions that urge themselves upon human beings arise? For Vico the main thing here is what in our contemporary terminology we would call the "humanization" of nature.

This refers to something of principal importance. Nature appears to us only in its meaning with reference to satisfying our existential needs. For this reason the decisive meaning of the function of work is given expression in Vico's interpretation of the myth of Hercules. The clearing of the primeval forest in order to delimit the first human place is the beginning of human history. No theory, no abstract philosophy is the origin of the human world, and every time that man loses contact with the original needs and the questions that arise out of them, he falls into the barbarism of *ratio*. "In this way, through long centuries of barbarism, rust will consume the misbegotten subtleties of malicious wits that have turned them into beasts. . . . Hence peoples who have reached this point of premeditated malice . . . are thereby stunned and brutalized. . . ."[11]

(d) But how does this "humanization of nature" take place

if not through *ratio*? We already said that nature possesses a meaning only in regard to human needs. This presupposes that we discover a relationship, a *similitudo*, between what the senses reveal to us and our needs. Already in classical Greek thought Pythagoras set forth the proposition that the similar can be grasped only through something similar [*similia similibus comprehendere*].

Insight into relationships basically is not possible through a process of inference, but rather only through an original *in*-sight as invention and discovery [*inventio*]. From this comes Vico's continual emphasis of *inventio* as primary over that which he calls "critical," i.e., purely rational thought.

Once again only insight into "common" or shared characteristics in the above-mentioned sense makes possible the lending of meanings that allow things to appear [*phainesthai*] in a way that is human. Since such a capacity is characteristic of fantasy, it is this, therefore, which lets the human world appear. For this reason it is expressed originally in metaphors, i.e., in the figurative lending of meanings. "Hence poetic wisdom, the first wisdom of the gentile world, must have begun with a metaphysics not rational and abstract like that of learned men now, but felt and imagined as that of these first men must have been, who, without power of ratiocination, were all robust sense and vigorous imagination." In another place Vico states: "The poetic characters of which we speak were certain imaginative genera . . . to which they reduced all the species or all the particulars appertaining to each genus."[12] Along these lines he also says: "Fantasy collects from the senses and connects and enlarges to exaggeration the sensory effects of natural appearances and makes luminous images from them, in order to suddenly blind the mind with lightning bolts and thereby to conjure up human passions in the ringing and thunder of this astonishment."[13]

The metaphor is, therefore, the original form of the interpretative act itself, which raises itself from the particular to the general through representation in an image, but, of course, always with regard to its importance for human beings. The Herculean act is always a metaphorical one and every genuine metaphor is in this sense Herculean work.

Two historical references can be given here which I can only mention. Seen from this standpoint there is a basic and very important parallelism concerning the original meaning of the structure and function of work between Vico and Marx. (I have developed this in my book *Humanismus und Marxismus*. [14]) In addition there is in this connection, within American philosophy, a striking relationship between Vico and the late Peirce.

As the fundamental result of this discussion we have (1) the primacy of "topical" philosophy ("topics" as the theory of the finding of arguments) over "rational" philosophy and (2) the primacy of rhetoric—as imagistic and effective speech and thereby dialogue—over rational speech and thereby over the monologue.

The Philosophical Importance of Cicero:
ingenium, inventio, usus, res

The question is now, in what tradition does Vico's view have its roots, his thesis of the priority of inventive, topical philosophy, of work as the source of the development of the human world through original ingenious activity? I want to answer this question with several references to Cicero, references through which the picture of Cicero as only a dilettantish popular thinker who repeated the ideas of Greek philosophers proves to be untenable and which bring to light his Roman-Latin originality.

Cicero conceives nature in two aspects. It is in its own way *mirabile*, hidden, and cannot be known in its most basic reality; it both excites our astonishment and puts before us tasks whereby it becomes the source of *invitamenta*. The second aspect of nature is that one that is revealed through human activity. Man transforms reality through his own capacities [*virtus*], "*magnus . . . vir et sapiens, cognovit, quae materies et quanta ad maximas res opportunitas in animis inesset hominum.*" [15]

These human capacities [*virtutes*] arise from *ingenium*, which Cicero calls "*semina virtutum.*" Through this ingenious activity we surpass what lies before us in our sensory awareness, "*Ingenii specimen est quoddam transilire ante pedes positum.*" Or in another formulation Cicero says: "*Magni autem est ingenii sevocare a sensibus,*" a statement that we find again almost word for word in Salutati's *De laboribus Herculis*. [16] The activity of *ingenium* consists in catching sight of relationships, of *similitudines* among things, "*Comparabile autem est, quod in rebus diversis similem aliquam rationem continet.*" This insight has no deductive character: "*Video summi ingenii causam esse,*" *non ut id demonstretur, quod ante oculos est.*"[17]

Cicero distinguishes in principle between the traditional art of proof, which is based upon deduction, and the art of invention. Since *ars demonstrandi* has no inventive character, "we find in this art no indication of how we are to find the truth [*nullum est praeceptum, quo modo inveniatur*], but only the way in which we are to judge [*sed tantum est quo modo iudicetur*]."[18]

An essential characteristic of *ingenium* consists in its *celeritas,* which is manifested in discerning, ingenious speech. It is ingenious activity that overcomes every "*dissidium . . . linguae atque cordis absurdum sane et inutile,*" a discrepancy that leads to the situation in which the "knower" is set on one side in opposition to the "person capable of speaking" [*alii nos sapere, alii dicere docerent*].[19] Cicero tries to eliminate this dualism which, in his opinion, is characteristic of Greek thought as a kind of philosophizing that is directed exclusively to the derivation of principles. Through what and in what form does nature make its appearance for man? It appears in the form of *res* as the carrier of human meanings, and it does this through work [*labor*]. By appearing as works within the limits that men have created, these *res* thereby are completed [*per-facere, perfectum*]. They receive their meaning in *usus.* In the *Orator* Cicero speaks of the "*doctos homines vel etiam usu peritos*"[20] and thereby emphasizes that the original human activity may not devote itself to "*res obscurae*" or "*non necessariae.*" Such an attitude, which is that of a purely formalistic thinking, is what Cicero goes so far as to call a "*vitium mentis*" because we must dedicate ourselves to those things that concern us immediately; these are the only things that constitute the original framework of our questions and answers.

Since the essence of *res* is revealed only in their ingenious utilization [*usus*] in the context of the social and political community, *res* proves to be *res publica,* and the state, in its concrete historical situation, turns out always to be its original horizon. Only with his efforts on the *res publica* does man grasp the deep meaning of his labor. In this way the "*magnus et sapiens vir*" raises the animal human being to something "new" within the limits of the community and unites him to a *populus.* In this theory of the *ingenium, virtus,* and labor the dichotomy of theory and praxis is *aufgehoben; ingenium* can never function in abstraction since it cannot manage "*sine rerum usu.*" *Ingenium* is revealed through work, through the alteration of the real with reference to human needs that present themselves in the real historical community. This means that the mind can be known exclusively through its own works.[21] To accomplish this act is what Vico calls "the act of Hercules"; it means both work and the taking of pains, which is the double meaning of the term "labor."

The historical aspects of the realization of the mind are *never eternally valid,* never absolutely "true," because they always emerge within limited situations bound in space and time; i.e., they are probable and seem to be true [*verisimile*], true only within the confines of "here" and "now," in which the needs and problems that confront human beings are met. I refer you here to the concept of *verisimile* as Vico develops it in his *On the Study Methods of Our Time* and in *De antiquissima Italorum sapientia.*

Cicero's Latin thought is fundamentally different from the medieval conception of knowledge, which proceeds through the derivation from original principles. Cicero conceived the only philosophical problems to be those that lead to the perfection of man within the context of situations that are always new. In this way Cicero came to the primacy of rhetoric, whose scientific significance is so resolutely denied by every variety of a priori thought. For when the *res* show their objective meaning through their utilization or *usus* with regard to their usefulness for society—and not for the individual—it follows from this that the orator, who speaks only in the context of different, particular situations, attains and expresses the meaning of the *res.* This is possible only when the *res* also are seen always as problems of the *res publica.*

On this interpretation the theoretical contemplative task is identical with the discovery of those forces that lie at the basis of the human world. Because man is no longer anchored within nature like the animals, he must discover the powers that have torn him out of nature and that force him to construct a world of his own.

The Reversal of the Traditional Interpretation of *contemplatio:* Vives's *Fabula de homine*

My task now would be to show how, on the basis of this tradition, the questions of the philosophical importance of philology, rhetoric, and jurisprudence are developed in the humanistic literature and how these come to be the basic structure of the human world. I have already almost completed this task elsewhere[22] and, therefore, want to direct my attention to another historical and theoretical perspective, which in my view has been given far too little attention from both the theoretical and historical point of view. I mean the view that emphasizes the theory of *ingenium* and results in a philosophical theory of metaphor.

I do not refer here to the Italian humanistic tradition, but to a Spanish representative of this movement, whereby we see also the historical breadth of the consciousness of these problems. I am referring to Juan Luis Vives (1492–1540). In his work the *Fabula de homine*,[23] we have a radical reversal of the medieval interpretation of metaphysics and a renunciation of the primacy of all speculation about nature, a disowning of every form of a priori or formal thinking—in line with the tradition that I have attempted to disclose here—as Vico formulated it, in order to look for the source of historicity in the modifications of the human mind.

Let me begin by noting that the traditional objects of *contemplatio* are the first principles and hence the eternal and unchanging from which we derive the meanings that we give to reality. In the *Fabula de homine* the object of thought is the changing, and from this the original and divine then are recognized. What is important here is the foundation. The mind—as the object of *contemplatio*—cannot show itself immediately, but only through different "masks," and it is here in fact that the principal similarity of man with the divine is revealed. Seeing this *similitudo*, the discovery of relationships between appearances as the foundation of the revelation of reality, is the task of the new ingenious philosophy.

Let us look at the *Fabula de homine* and the way it is written and how it reverses the concept of *contemplatio*. In it, according to a schéma to which the Italian humanists turn again and again (it is enough to recall Giordano Bruno's *Spaccio della bestia trionfante*), we have a "fantastic" story of a festival on Olympus to celebrate Juno's birthday. A "theater performance"—let us not forget this—takes place. The aim of this undertaking is that man is invited to show or act out for the others his threefold nature: vegetable, sensitive, and intellectual. Man fulfills his task in such a perfected way that, as Vives puts it, the gods are filled with doubt, for possibly Jupiter himself is acting under the masks of these men. "When the gods first saw him, they were roused and upset at the thought that their master and father had stooped to the stage [*hunc simul ac dii conspicati sunt, primum animo commoti atque turbati dominum putarunt patremque suum in scenam descendisse*]."[24] The amazement at this play which overcame the gods is so extreme that they check to see if Jupiter is still in the audience. "Soon, however, with composed minds, they glanced repeatedly at Jupiter's stall wondering whether he himself was still sitting there or whether he had appeared masked to play a part [*post vero, sedata mente, oculos identidem ad Iovis sellam tollebant, ut viderent sederetne illic ipse, an personatus prodiiset aliquid acturus*]."[25]

According to the general opinion of interpreters, the parallelism between this elevation of man and that found in *De Hominis Dignitate* of Pico della Mirandola or Giannozzo Manetti's work of the same name is what must be taken into account. But de facto I do not believe that this exhausts the philosophical content of Vives's fable. I believe its accent comes from the fact that, when compared with the views of Pico and Manetti, it represents a complete reversal of intepretations concerning knowledge that is based upon *contemplatio*.

Let us remember that in Vives's text the concern is viewing not merely a theater performance, i.e., a *contemplatio*, but also a *fabula*, that is, a form which, according to humanist tradition, lays claim to revealing a truth in a disguise.[26] With such an interpretation the fable no longer can be seen as merely a "game" of fantasy, as a purely literary jest. Let us remember here again that we also are dealing with *seeing* a theater performance (in Greek *theoria*, in Latin *contemplatio*) that is put on by gods and not men. Not only that, it takes place on the occasion of a celebration, that is, this *theoria* takes place at a time that represents the pinnacle of existence, the high point of joy, freedom, and perfection.

In the course of this "fabulous" story there is a *peristrophe*, to use a term from Aristotle's analysis of drama, that is of theatrical action [*drao*]. At the beginning of the fable the gods are *viewers*, but in the course of the play they recognize themselves as put into the play, that is, they no longer stand before the stage, before the drama. Instead it is the other way around; the play proves to be original reality. The play is performed and the gods recognize themselves in this human work. "O great Jupiter, what a spectacle for them! At first they were astonished that they, too, should be brought to the stage and impersonated by such a convincing mime, whom they said to be that multiform Proteus, the son of Ocean [*Primum, stupescere se in scenam etiam introductos, expressosque ab hoc tam Ethico mimo, quem plerique multiformem illum Protheum Oceani filium esse affirmabant*]."[27]

The gods recognize themselves in the acting, in man's concrete development, because his divinity becomes visible in this sphere. What was at first a play and fiction changes into "reality," and it is this *peristrophé* which in fact induces the gods to invite man to leave the scene, to put down his mask, and to sit with them. "They prevailed upon Jupiter, through Juno's intercession, that man, who had so rightly played the parts of Jupiter and the gods, *put off his mask* and be seated among the gods [. . . *homo, qui deorum et Jovis personas tam apte egisset, persona deposita, inter deos sederet*]."[28]

The fable, the fantastic representation of a truth, is the original form of man's self-realization in Vives's view. Here it is legitimized methodologically as the expression of a truth under a disguise (the human mask). At bottom here is a similarity [*similitudo*] between the community of man with what is primordial. "Man lay bare, showing the immortal gods his nature akin to theirs" [*ostendit agnationem illam quam habet cum diis*].[29] Vico's statement that man should not concern himself with the study of nature but rather ought to direct his study to history is anticipated here.

Necessitas and *Ingenium* as the Origin of the Community

With respect to what we said at the beginning of our discussion about Vico, we must recall that we could point out fundamental ideas in Vives that we had emphasized in Cicero and in Vico. On the one hand the human world stands as the expression of needs that are to be fulfilled, and on the other hand it represents the efforts of an ingenious capacity. The noteworthy element here is the continuity of this basic theme and problem, a continuity which most of all comes from the nature of the question itself and its examination. For example we have no reason to assume that Vico knew the writings of Vives. A few indications of this are found in the fact that for Vives there are two sources of society, the word and justice, "*societas ipsa per se sine iustitia et sermone stare omnino non potest. . . . Humanae omnes societates, duabus potissimum rebus vinciuntur ac continentur, iustitia, et sermone.*"[30]

Justice has a slow, quiet power, while the word possesses a

pressing and quick force that affects both the mind and the passions. *"Iustitia tacitas habet vires, et lentas, sermo vero praesentiores, et magis celeres, quod alter rationis et consilii vim admonet, alter animi modus excitat."* This is precisely the reason why the orator assumes such an important place in society, for Vives defines the word as "the living flow of the soul [*esse in animi fluvio sermone*]."[31]

The origin of society, history, work, the arts, and metaphor, however, is the *inventio,* which overcomes man's difficult situation, *"Prima rerum inventio necessitati succurrit."* In another place Vives says, *"Ita artibus, quae praesenti atque urgenti necessitati opem ferrent, rite inventis ac constitutis."* The fact is that the circumstances in which particular urgent needs arise are new and will not be repeated and, to use Vives's metaphor, "besiege us," they sharpen our inventive capacity. *"Haec [necessitas] enim ingenia mirifice exacuit ad ea excudenda, quibus obsessor adeo gravis arceatur."*[32]

Vives defines *ingenium* precisely as that capacity in man which can meet urgent needs through its acumen. *"Ingenii acumen vivax, et sua sponte actuosum: hinc sunt nata inventa hominum omnia, utilia, noxia, proba, improba."* Even the metaphor, that figurative transfer of meaning, stands in the service of satisfying urgent needs. *"Ornatius dicendi et acutius inveniendi, ex necessitate fluxit."*[33]

Ingenious Activity in Mannerism

These doctrines that we have sought to reveal in their own contexts prove to be influential on subsequent humanist thought. Illustrative of this is their decisive importance for the theoreticians of the so-called Mannerist movement. We want to leave open the question of whether for these Mannerists the theory of *ingenium* and metaphor fulfilled an ontological or literary function. But it is important to note that this problem appears again here in a new context and to direct our inquiry from this standpoint to the Mannerists. In this tradition the basic problem is what capacity lies at the basis of "insight" into relationships as the ingenious act which is presupposed by metaphor? The Mannerist authors define ingenious activity as "acuteness" [*argutezza* or *acutezza*] with reference to the fact that in this way they are able to gain access to the deepest essence of that which manifests itself. *Argutezza* is derived etymologically from the root *arg,* which is found in Greek *argyros* "silver" and *enarges* "distinct," as well as in Latin *argentum* "silver," that is, it is used for the designation of something that stands out because of its brilliance.[34]

In this interpretation of *ingenium* Aristotle's doctrine of the metaphor is taken as the basis. Emmanuele Tesauro (1591–1675), who named his programmatic main work *The Aristotelian Telescope*, claims that "what I say here agrees in large part with what the classical teachers of antiquity said . . . including among others the opinion of Aristotle, who maintains . . . that seeing relationships [*convenienza*] between the most distant things is proper to acuteness and *ingenium*." Therefore, what ingenious activity provides by virtue of its combinations is "a theater full of wonders" [*teatro pieno di mirabilie*],[35] a "theater," a "performance" of wonders, that takes place before human beings.

Tesauro emphasizes the social character of ingenious expressions; he calls the subject matter of genius "*materia civile*"[36] insofar as these acute expressions are directed to honor, mutual help, and justice, i.e., to those things that determine man's life in a community. Man would use up his energies in the purely rational search for truth because then "the mind is melancholy and lonesome." For this reason acuteness and wit assume a decisive role; the acute expression represents the dignity of urban men.[37]

The purely aesthetic theory of *ingenium* then is restricted to a new reality—the poetic—which is transformed through metaphor but which is taken to serve only as diversion and distraction from the immediate historical tasks and hence to be in no way binding. This interpretation seems to follow Tesauro when he asserts that the doctrine of ingenious speech arose out of a struggle against the boredom of the purely rational monologue. "Like all ornaments that serve our amusement and bring variety to the purely functional aspect of ships, walls, and vases—which are called '*schemata*' in Greek and '*figurae*' in Latin—all those which drive away the boredom of the listener, words, sentences, and inferences that are distinguished from bare ordinary expressions, are called rhetorical schema and figures."[38]

In a polemic against purely rational speech he adds, "Men experience this supersaturation in rational speech . . . so that they listen to deep and beneficial doctrines with yawns and sleepiness whenever wit and the newness of the game to which *ingenium* spurs them on, does not keep them awake."[39] In the same way Giovanni Pellegrini (1595–1652) distinguishes in his two works *Delle acutezze che altrimenti spiriti, vivezze, concetti volgarmente si appellano* (1639) and *Fonti dell' ingenio* (1650) among origin, essence, and types of wit. This consists in combining in a new way not only words but things as well [*il loro vicendevole collegamento*], hence making them evident to us.[40] Significantly Pellegrini mentions three kinds of "putting in combination" or connecting. The first is that of a proposition in which something of that kind takes place but without giving a reason for it, in other words a pure assertion. The second is that kind which gives the basis of the assertion or connection. "This is the procedure that the logicians generally call a syllogism." The third consists in showing something completely "new" and in itself underivable which is "created" by means of discovering relationships.[41]

We should note also that in his work *Agudeza y arte de ingenio,* the great theoretician of Mannerism, Gracián (1601–1658), criticizes the fact that classical antiquity primarily directed its attention to the syllogism, i.e., to the rational process. "They have recognized wit and acuteness but they have not really evaluated it; they were satisfied with marveling at it and did not investigate it."[42]

In the theory of *concepto*—this concept comes to Mannerism from the term *conceptualismo*—the topic is conceptualization or "combination" that arises through the creation of relations between completely different phenomena that are far removed from one another; it has nothing to do with the deduction of a logical essence. *Concepto* is defined literally as "immediate phenomenon," as the creation of a "harmonic relation between two or three external objects of knowledge [*primorosa correlación entre dos o tres cognoscibles externos*]." Accordingly Gracián defines the activity of *ingenium* as an "act of insight that expresses the relationship that holds between two objects."[43] *Ingenium* is the sphere of wit and acuteness.[44] The main task of *ingenium* is to "decipher" the world[45] without which reality would remain unknown and mute; *ingenium* is hence an activity that lets the divine shine.

Once man has emerged from the "cave of nature," as Gracián puts it in his *Criticón,* he must learn to see new relationships and to realize them through his behavior. He is able to accomplish this by being confronted with his historicity and its falsifications. The negativity of the historical world that is unfolded before the protagonist of Gracián's novel is not an expression of the author's pessimism but an intentional pedagogical confrontation with the dangers of the "new" world in order to educate man dialectically.

I have attempted to suggest how the humanistic tradition is rooted in the Latin tradition and is differentiated in a fundamental way from a priori thought on the one hand and every type of formalism on the other. This scholarly tradition is continued in Pontano, Landino, Poliziano, Valla, and Nizolio. The problems of this tradition were continued in modern thought in England with the theory of *ingenium,* wit, common sense, and the affirmation of rhetorical, metaphorical speech in Shaftesbury and then in Germany in the eighteenth century in the polemical, anti-idealistic thought of Hamann, Jean Paul, and Herder.

Rhetoric and Philosophy

The Primacy of Rhetorical Speech

The problem of rhetoric—as the speech that acts on the emotions—can be treated from two points of view. It can be considered simply as a doctrine of a type of speech that the traditional rhetors, politicians, and preachers need, i.e., only as an art, as a technique of persuading. In this case the problems of rhetoric will be limited to questions of practical directions for persuading people and will not have a theoretical character.

From another point of view, however, the problems of rhetoric can be seen as involving a relation to philosophy, to theoretical speech. We can formulate this in the following way: If philosophy aims at being a theoretical mode of thought and speech, can it have a rhetorical character and be expressed in rhetorical forms? The answer seems obvious. Theoretical thinking, as a rational process, excludes every rhetorical element because pathetic influences—the influences of feeling—disturb the clarity of rational thought.

Locke and Kant, for example, express this view, and their statements are characteristic of the rationalistic attitude toward rhetoric. Locke writes:

> I confess, in discourses where we seek rather pleasure and delight than information and improvement, such ornaments as are borrowed from them can scarce pass for faults. But yet if we would speak of things as they are, we must allow that all the art of rhetoric, besides order and clearness; all the artificial and figurative application of words eloquence hath invented, are for nothing else but to insinuate wrong ideas, move the passions, and thereby mislead the judgment; and so are perfect cheats.[1]

Kant writes:

> Rhetoric, so far as this is taken to mean the art of persuasion, i.e., the art of deluding by means of a fair semblance [as *ars oratoria*], and not merely excellence of

speech (eloquence and style), is a dialectic, which borrows from poetry only so much as is necessary to win over men's minds to the side of the speaker before they have weighed the matter, and to rob their verdict of its freedom. . . . Force and elegance of speech (which together constitute rhetoric) belong to fine art; but oratory [*ars oratoria*], being the art of playing for one's own purpose upon the weaknesses of men (let this purpose be ever so good in intention or even in fact) merits no *respect* whatever.[2]

It is obvious that the problem of rhetoric as conceived here places philosophy in a position preeminent to rhetoric. Rhetoric is seen only as a technical doctrine of speech. Only the clarification of rhetoric in its relation to theoretical thought can allow us to delimit the function of rhetoric. Only this will allow us to decide whether rhetoric has a purely technical, exterior, and practical aim of persuading, or whether it has an essentially philosophical structure and function.

The solution to this problem can be worked out only if we establish the following fact: We claim that we know something when we are able to prove it. To prove [*apo-deiknumi*] means to *show* something to be something, on the basis of something. To have something through which something is shown and explained definitively is the foundation of our knowledge. Apodictic, demonstrative speech is the kind of speech which establishes the definition of a phenomenon by tracing it back to ultimate principles, or *archai*. It is clear that the first *archai* of any proof and hence of knowledge cannot be proved themselves because they cannot be the object of apodictic, demonstrative, logical speech; otherwise they would not be the first assertions. Their nonderivable, primary character is evident from the fact that we neither can speak nor comport ourselves without them, for both speech and human activity simply presuppose them. But if the original assertions are not demonstrable, what is the character of the speech in which we express them? Obviously this type of speech cannot have a rational-theoretical character.

In other words it is evident that the rational process and consequently rational speech must move from the formulation of primary assertions. Here we are confronted with the fundamental question of the character necessary to the formulation of basic premises. Evidently by using this kind of expression, which belongs to the original, to the nondeducible, they cannot have an apodictic, demonstrative character and structure but are thoroughly *indicative*. It is only the indicative character of *archai* that makes demonstration possible at all.

The indicative or allusive {*semeinein*} speech provides the framework within which the proof can come into existence. Furthermore if rationality is identified with the process of clarification, we are forced to admit that the primal clarity of the principles is not rational and recognize that the corresponding language in its indicative structure has an "evangelic" character, in the original Greek sense of this word, i.e., "noticing."

Such speech is immediately a "showing"—and for this reason "figurative" or "imaginative," and thus in the original sense "theoretical" {*theorein*—i.e., to see}. It is metaphorical, i.e., it shows something which has a sense, and this means that to the figure, to that which is shown, the speech transfers {*metapherein*} a signification; in this way the speech which realizes this showing "leads before the eyes" {*phainesthai*} a significance. This speech is and must be in its structure an imaginative language.

If the image, the metaphor, belongs to rhetorical speech (and for this reason it has a pathetic character), we also are obliged to recognize that every original, former, "archaic" speech (archaic in the sense of dominant, *arche, archomai; archontes* or the dominants) cannot have a rational but only a rhetorical character. Thus the term "rhetoric" assumes a fundamentally new significance; "rhetoric" is not, nor can it be the art, the technique of an exterior persuasion; it is rather the speech which is the basis of the rational thought.

This original speech, because of its "archaic" character, sketches the framework for every rational consideration, and for this reason we are obliged to say that rhetorical speech "comes before" every rational speech, i.e., it has a "prophetic" {*pro-phainesthai*} character and never again can be comprehended from a rational, deductive point of view. This is the tragedy of the rationalistic process.

Furthermore knowledge, or the explanation of something through its cause, constitutes a process which is as such of a temporal nature, for as something that has happened it is a historical phenomenon which has passed through different moments in time. The primary speech instead reveals itself instantaneously {*exaiphnes*}. It does not lie within historical time; it is the origin and criterion of the movement of the rational process of clarification.

If the essence of the speech, which expresses the original, has to be purely semantic, because it is only through this kind of speech that the demonstrative language becomes at all possible, we must distinguish between two kinds of language: the *rational language,* which is dialectical, mediating, and demonstrative, i.e., apodictic and without any pathetic character, and the *semantic language,* which is immediate, not deductive or demonstrative, illuminating, purely indicative, and which has a preeminence opposite the rational language. On the basis of its figurative, metaphorical character, this language has an original pathetic essence.

This is the reason why only from a formal point of view the original, immediate, purely semantic word belongs necessarily to the sacred, religious word, while the mediating, step-by-step, demonstrating and proof-giving (apodictic) word is covered by the rational and historical word.

Now we are in a position to understand the meaning of a sentence of Heraclitus who, at the beginning of the Western tradition, expressed what we have taken to develop here: "The lord to whom the oracle of Delphi belongs says nothing and conceals nothing; he indicates, shows [*oute legei oute kruptei alla semainei;* fr. B 93]."

Cassandra's Tragic Movement from Rhetoric to Rationality

The consciousness of all these problems—the admission of the structure of original language as not rational but rhetorical; the interpretation of rhetoric primarily not as an expression of an art of conviction but as an expression of the original and, in this sense, of the religious speech with its "evangelic" and "prophetic" character; and finally the admission that through rational language and thought, we never comprehend the primary and original thought and speech—all these points are expressed in the tragedy of Cassandra in the *Agamemnon* of Aeschylus.

I wish to develop what I have said previously by interpreting the Greek text that, from this point of view and in this manner, demonstrates the original framework in which the Greeks have treated, in a nonrational manner, the problem of original rhetorical speech and its original philosophical dimension.

The background of Cassandra's personal tragedy is well known. She was chosen as mistress by Apollo and promised to yield to him if he would grant her, in exchange, the gift of prophecy. Having received this gift she denied herself to the god, who thereupon punished her by depriving her of her sight and providing that no one in the future should believe in her prophecies or understand her utterances.

Who is Cassandra? Homer mentions her in the *Iliad* as the daughter of the king of Troy, but he does not elaborate on her fatal gift of prophecy (*Iliad* 13. 366, 24. 699). Pindar describes her as a prophet (*Pyth.* 11. 20). Factually, of the texts that have come down to us, the *Agamemnon* provides the final comprehensive interpretation of the Cassandra figure; the gravity of her "external" tragedy rests on the myth of Apollo and his beloved. But is Aeschylus merely concerned with this story, or does he have in mind a tragedy that lies deeper and points to a fundamental phenomenon of human existence?

How is Cassandra's semantic language constructed? At the beginning of the Cassandra tragedy one can see already that the Chorus is trying in vain to enter into a dialogue with the seer. Here its first reaction is the reproach that Cassandra's invocation of the god Apollo as well as the way she invoked him were unseemly; it considers her exclamation senseless and improper. Cassandra does not hear the words of the Chorus; she repeats her invocation (v. 1076), and again the Chorus reacts in a rational manner (v. 1078). Once more Cassandra takes no notice of it. Until the passage referred to previously, the Chorus will at no price give up the attempt to enter into a conversation with Cassandra; in the same measure it refuses to alter its own explanatory attitude.

The contrast between Cassandra and the Chorus is obvious; each moves in a space and in a time of its own. The Chorus moves in the realm of expoundable rationality and in a time which makes the future appear simply as a *possibility*. It speaks, in the text, in the grammatical form used for reporting the past. Its language, therefore, is temporal, in the sense that it attempts to grasp and to reflect the unfolding of events and their relations.

Cassandra's space, on the other hand, is determined by the simultaneous nature of the vision in which the movements of time are fused, and turn into parts of an immovable, necessary, and no longer merely possible instant. In accordance with her "seer's" gifts Cassandra speaks a pictorial language which is distinguished from that of the Chorus by frequently falling back on participial phrases. The contrast between the world of Cassandra and that of the Chorus definitely illustrates the fact that the semantic approach cannot be attained or derived through a logical process.

Never does an explanatory word pass over Cassandra's lips, for she herself knows nothing of cause and effect. She speaks only through images and symbols. Death itself is symbolized by a net in which the animal (bull or cow, as a metaphor for Agamemnon) will be ensnared; the ruse, the snare, "dawns" upon him ("What is it? What appears there? / A fishing-net of Hades? A snare to catch the husband, an accomplice for / the murder") (v. 1115).

In the second main passage (vv. 1136–1214) the transition takes place from Cassandra's ecstatic, mantic condition to her human sphere; rational elements come into the foreground and thus provide the beginning of a dialogical relation between Cassandra and the Chorus. How does this transition occur? Cassandra begins with a lament about her own death, though here she still addresses the god rather than the Chorus. In this speech she no longer asks the god where she is, as she did at the beginning of her appearance on stage, but *why* he has led her hither. So for the first time she asks for an *explanation,* a reason for her being here (v. 1138). By entering the plane of *explanation* and abandoning the world of allusion with this question, she causes her historical reality to be outlined, and she herself moves into a historical framework of time and space.

The manner in which the poet lures Cassandra from her purely semantic and mantic plane into the rational historical world, and thus makes it possible for the Chorus to enter into a dialogue with her, is characteristic and significant. This conversational passage becomes a sign of her departure from the world of the inexplicable, the original, the purely semantic. The change is brought about through a *metaphor,* as though this were the only possible bridge between the rational and the semantic realms. The Chorus compares her complaints with those of Prokne, the nightingale (v. 1140). This *image* touches Cassandra in her longing for the human world to which she originally belonged, and at the same time touches her in connection with her impending lot. *For the first time,* stimulated by this *image,* Cassandra hears the words of the Chorus and reacts to them (v. 1146).

The question which the Chorus now asks Cassandra, and the ensuing conversation (that is, the beginning of a dialogue between the protagonist of the semantic, original world and that of the rational, proving world of the Chorus) is founded on an image, a metaphor. This metaphor has an emotional impact and appeals to a longing—a human passion—which lures the human being standing in the semantic realm into the world of explanation, of occurrence, of sequence, in other words, into the realm of time dominated by death. In the purely semantic sphere there was merely the presence of images, of indications; there was a lack of causal explanations. In accordance with this abrupt change Cassandra's language also changes; suddenly she uses the past form indispensably within a perspective involving time (v. 1158).

Lured by the images of the past Cassandra also talks about her relation with Apollo (v. 1202). The text does not justify the assumption that it was love that made Cassandra promise herself to the god, but rather that she did it with an ulterior motive. She wanted to receive the gift warranted by the god's possession of her, by the fusion with him, the divine ecstasy of the prophet which eliminates the order of the temporal sequence of cause and effect and also rational speech. The divine gift—to encompass all in an instant—is something Cassandra desired not for herself alone; she wanted to communicate it to others, to be mediator between the divine and the human. However, her real aim was to obtain the gift *through a ruse*. Ruse is rational design, and no rational process or attitude can ever lead to the origins of being, to the divine, for the divine conditions the rational process.

The tragedy of Cassandra, the curse pursuing her, is based on her rationality, odd though that may sound. Since it is impossible to grasp the divine by rational methods, a failure to recognize this fact becomes a cure. Rationality also prevents the Chorus from having any communication, any dialogue, with Cassandra while she is still on a semantic plane. Her figure is uncanny because it is her rational intention to communicate timelessness to the historical and rational world; men lack the means to understand her pronouncements and illuminations by way of reason. This access can be opened only through images, metaphor, semantic speech. The "seeing" thus gains absolute precedence over the other senses in semantic language.

The Relation of Rhetoric to the Rational Process

Let us consider the rational, logical process more closely. The fruitfulness of any deductions obviously grows out of the fruitfulness of the premises; the more productive the premises, the more productive the deductions. The validity and framework of the conclusions depend on the validity and framework of the premises.

If we question this conception of the rational process as to the kind of premises from which the syllogism or the deduction set out, we again come up against the *archai*, "the principles." Here we have to remember the original meaning of *arche* and of the verb *archomai*, "to lead, to guide, to rule." To lead or to guide was expressed in Latin as *inducere* and in Greek as *epagein*. From this we can derive that "principles" alone can be the only true and original point of departure, the real foundation of induction, of *epagoge* as the process of reducing the multiplicity to a unity; therefore the real and valid concept of induction cannot be identified with a process that has its point of departure in the multiplicity and arises to a unity through abstraction.

Aristotle, in his meditation about the essence of the logical process and its inevitable premises, gives the term *pistis* or "faith," "belief" (which is so important in rhetoric), a meaning which was forgotten completely and which no longer coincides with the meaning of *doxa*, much less with the special form of rational conviction founded on proof. In the *Posterior Analytics* Aristotle defines knowledge and conviction, that is, the *rational* belief [*pistis*] arising from conviction, as "One believes and knows something when a deduction is carried out which we call proof" (*Anal. post. 72a 25*). It is clear that Aristotle here assigns a rational character to the concept of *pistis*, conviction, understanding, and knowledge [*eidenai*] from a special perspective; the determining factor is *deduction*. Proof consists in "giving the reason." The reason becomes evident in connection with the deduction, which necessarily starts from premises and hence depends on their validity.

Aristotle continues: "Since the conclusion obtains its true validity from the fact that the reason on which it is based is evident, it necessarily follows that with each proof, the first principles in which it has origin must not only be known completely or partially prior to the proof, they must *also be known to a higher degree* than that which is deduced from them" (*Anal. post. 72a 27*).

So when we *know* and *believe* in connection with a proof, we must necessarily *believe* and *know* the premises on which the proof is based *on more forceful grounds*. Aristotle accentuates this fundamental condition: "If we *know and believe* an object by means of the first principle to a more forceful degree than that which is derived from it, *we know and believe* the latter on the basis of the first" (*Anal. post.* 72a 30).

Are we conscious of the change in the meaning of knowledge and belief, as expressed in this passage? Hitherto there has been mention only of a belief, and knowledge and belief, which is more primary than the rational form and of necessity radically different in structure. We must remember, nevertheless, that the nonrational character of the principles is by no means identical with irrationality; the necessity and universal validity in the nonrational character of the *archai* impose themselves equally or to a higher degree than the universal validity and necessity effective in the deductive process and resting on the foundation of strict logic.

It seems useful to quote another Aristotelian passage: "The principles—all or some—must necessarily be lent *more belief* than what is deduced. He who arrives at a certain knowledge through proof must necessarily . . . *know and believe the principles to a higher degree than what is deduced from them*" (*Anal. post.* 72a 37). The task resulting from this consists in a further elucidation of the structure of this knowledge and belief, and this task belongs to the problems resulting from the relation between philosophical and rhetorical speech. Here we must point out the following: The *techne* of rhetoric, as the art of persuasion, of forming belief, structures the emotive framework which creates the tension within which words, questions that are dealt with, and actions that are discussed, acquire their passionate significance. It creates a tension through which the audience is literally "sucked into" the framework designed by the author.

The emotive word affects us through its directness. Since emotional life unrolls in the framework of directly indicative signs, a word must evoke these signs in order to relieve or to soothe the passions. As a passionate, and not exclusively rational, being, man is in need of the emotive word.

So over the centuries, under the aspect of the relationship between *content* and *form*, the thesis was again and again developed that images and rhetoric were to be appreciated primarily from outside, for *pedagogical reasons*, that is, as aids to "alleviate" the "severity" and "dryness" of rational language. To resort to images and metaphors, to the full set of implements proper to rhetoric and artistic language, in this sense, merely serves to make it "easier" to absorb rational truth.

Therefore rhetoric generally was assigned a *formal* function, whereas philosophy, as *episteme*, as rational knowledge, was to supply the true, factual content. This distinction is significant because the essence of man is determined both by logical and emotional elements, and as a result speech can reach the human being as a union of *logos* and *pathos* only if it appeals to both these aspects.

A statement of this kind carries important implications: (1) The only true educational method, the only true way of teaching, is rational deduction and demonstration, which can be taught and learned in its rules and its proceedings. Education is based on explanation. (2) Attestation loses its significance altogether; the only valid testimony is the logical process. Its structure is conditioned by the rationality of proof. Problems, so-called problems of form and style, which cannot be identified with the structure of rational demonstration, are rhetorical and not theoretical, i.e., they are external. In other words the rational content determines the form; in the realm of theoretical thought there exists no problem of form which can be divorced from the rational content. (3) Knowledge is unhistorical in its essence because logical evidence *always* is valid when it has been acknowledged on the basis of its necessity and universal validity, which it possesses by definition. The historical character of knowledge at most may be of significance as regards a reconstruction of the process leading to knowledge. (4) Every cognition is necessarily *anonymous* because the rational grounds, with their necessity and universal validity, are not bound up with individual persons.

But is this conception of pedagogy which involves a determined theory of rhetoric valid? Has it not been shown already that the original, archaic (in the sense which I gave to this term) assertions have in their structure a belief, a figurative, imaginative character, so that every original speech is in its aim illuminating and persuading? In this original speech evidently it is impossible to separate content and form and also, in pedagogical terms, to look for a "posterior" unity of them.

Plato's Union of Knowledge and Passion

Now I wish to clarify the relations between rhetoric and philosophy with reference to classical antiquity; my aim is to find out whether the need was felt, and if so, in what manner, to establish a union between knowledge and passion, a union that can be reached neither through the external emotive disguise of a rational "content," nor through pouring a rational content into an emotive "form." To this end let us consider Plato's dialogues the *Gorgias* and the *Phaedrus*. An examination of what I consider a misinterpretation of Plato regarding the dualism between rhetoric and philosophy will be helpful in classifying the problem.

According to the traditional interpretation Plato's attitude against rhetoric is a rejection of the *doxa,* or opinion, and of the impact of images, upon which the art of rhetoric relies; at the same time his attitude is considered as a defense of the theoretical, rational speech, that is, of *episteme.* The fundamental argument of Plato's critique of rhetoric usually is exemplified by the thesis, maintained, among other things, in the *Gorgias,* that only he who "knows" [*epistatai*] can speak correctly; for what would be the use of the "beautiful," of the rhetorical speech, if it merely sprang from opinions [*doxa*], hence from not knowing? This interpretation of Plato's attitude in his dialogue *Gorgias,* however, fails to take account of some unmistakable factual difficulties.

His rejection of rhetoric, when understood in this manner, assumes that Plato rejects every emotive element in the realm of knowledge. But in several of his dialogues Plato connects the philosophical process, for example, with *eros,* which would lead to the conclusion that he attributes a decisive role to the emotive, seen even in philosophy as the absolute science. So we will have to ask ourselves how those apparently contradictory tenets are to be explained and to what extent the essence of philosophy is not exhausted for Plato in the *episteme,* i.e., in the typical rational process it requires. Will we find here a deeper meaning of rhetoric?

Plato's *Gorgias* comes to terms with the claims of rhetorical art. Gorgias here supports the thesis that rhetoric can rightly claim "to carry out and fulfil *everything* through speech" (451d). How shall we interpret this "everything"? Gorgias's answer is: The greatest and most important of all things human, that is, health, richness, beauty; to attain all that belongs to the aim of rhetoric. But is rhetoric capable of attaining these gifts of mankind? The physician, for example, will deny that anyone can be cured merely through speech, without special knowledge. What then is the use of the art of convincing, of *peithein?* So Socrates decides to find out "what kind of persuasion is the kind accomplished by the art of rhetoric" (453c).

He comes to distinguish between true and false belief (454d 5) and proves that in contradiction to belief, to *doxa,* there can be no true or false *episteme* or rational knowledge because it is rooted in grounds, in reasons. As a result rational knowledge [*episteme*] and rational speech is superior; it admits no form of opinion besides itself, no form that is not covered by founded knowledge. Since rhetoric does not convince by means of such rational knowledge, it remains always in the realm of pseudo-knowledge.

This radically negative judgment of rhetoric traditionally is considered to be Plato's definitive attitude to rhetoric, and that in view of the thesis that rational knowledge, i.e., philosophy, represents the only true and valid rhetorical art. This, however, leaves the problem of the relationship between passion, instinct, and the rational process unsolved. The belief inspired in man on the basis of emotive speeches accordingly would have to yield to rational knowledge, or be canceled by it; but knowledge alone, as a rational process, can neither move the human being nor carry him away to certain actions.

Gorgias answers Socrates with the following objection: Of what use is all the physician's knowledge if the patient does not pluck up courage to do what the physician has prescribed? So one does need rhetoric. A similar objection: A community rarely opts for what the specialist advises, but rather for what a capable orator proposes. The dilemma we perceived earlier seems insurmountable; on one side, there is an ineffectual rational knowledge, on the other speech as pure "seduction." Therefore how can we resolve the problem?

The problem of the *pathos* (and with it, of rhetoric) in its relationship to theoretical, i.e., epistemic, speech forms the central theme of the *Phaedrus,* the second dialogue with which I propose to deal. Its first part, as is well known, concerns *eros.* Phaedrus (a disciple of the rhetorician Lycias) holds a speech against *eros.* The subsequent speech of Socrates is equally directed against *eros* and so against *pathos;* suddenly, however, Socrates stops short. Since he is ashamed of having spoken against *eros,* he holds a third speech, which develops into a praise of *eros.*

These three speeches on *eros* are followed by the second part of the dialogue, which has as its subject the nature and structure of rhetoric and begins with a solemn reference to the Muses, in connection with a myth, namely, of the cicadas. The cicadas, Socrates explains, originally descended from human beings who lived before the time of the Muses. When the Muses were conceived and began to sing, a few of these human beings were so enthralled by them that they forgot about food and only wanted to sing, so that they almost died unnoticed. These lovers of Muses were turned into cicadas; their task was to report to the Muses, after their death, who among humans was most devoted to which one of the Muses, and Socrates comes to speak about the Muse of philosophy (259d 3). In general, as we have seen, a speech is called "philosophical" when it is based on a knowledge of reasons. Statements based on knowledge possess a rational character; they belong to the field of *episteme,* of theoretical thought. But rational speech itself, as we know, starts out from premises that are not rational because they are based on first affirmations. The rational process *does* forbid the insertion of any element connected with the Muses. But if Plato, as for example in *Gorgias,* identifies the only art of convincing which he accepts, with rational knowledge, i.e., *episteme,* how are we to understand the fact that here he places philosophy under the sign of the Muses? Is it only a casual reference?

We can answer this question only when we ask: What is the meaning of the condition of man *before* the birth of the Muses? Why should men have been so fascinated by the Muses and their work that they went so far as to forget about food, and what has this to do with philosophy?

We cannot develop here the different meanings and interpretations of the Muses. The problem is why Plato, in his *Phaedrus,* refers to the Muses with his myth of the cicadas, speaking of the essence and structure of philosophy and what he meant by the condition of men *before* the creation of the "Muses" and their "enraptured" condition after the appearance of these goddesses. What relation can there be between the work of Muses and philosophy?

The meaning of the word "muse" remains unknown. Attempts at an etymological derivation of the term began in classical times, namely, with Plato. In the *Cratylus* he says: "The Muses, however, and music in general, were evidently thus named by Apollo from *musing* [*moosthai*]" (406a). The word *moosthai* contains in its implication a process of *searching,* of "storm and stress." Plutarch, in addition to his derivation of the word from *homou ousai* "existing at once, simultaneously," whereby he points to their union (*De fraterno amore* 6), also mentions a second one, which he considers a result of the analogy between *mousai* and *mneiai,* those who remember (*Quaest. conv.* 9.14).

In the activities of the Muses, the concept of order clearly plays a prevalent and unifying part. The order of *movements* appears in the dance, the order of *tones* in song, and the order of *words* in verse. Furthermore order is the starting point of *rhythm* and *harmony*. Plato says in the *Laws:* "The order of movement is named *rhythm,* the order of voice, of the connection between high and low tones, is called *harmony*" (665a).

The reference made in the *Laws* to the "order of movement" seems particularly significant because movement represents a fundamental phenomenon in the realm of existence; whatever is perceived through the senses shows a *becoming,* that is, a movement in itself (change) or a movement in space. Through the application of a *measure,* movement proceeds within certain barriers and under certain laws; it is, as one might put it, "arranged." Thus we can understand how numbers, as expressions of measure, of proportions in arts, were originally given a religious significance, and also we can understand the sacred character of dance, song, and music. Plato complains in the *Laws* about the decadence of the arts insofar as they are no longer a manifestation of the original, objective harmony. This complaint refers to the decadence of the *mousike,* which is not only music but the union of song, verse, and dance in their original objectiveness (*Laws* 700 d–e). The Muses, on the contrary, represent the link with the objective, which makes the original order of the human world possible in the face of the arbitrary, the subjective, the relative, and the changeable. The reference to the ground in which knowledge, *episteme,* is anchored is a remembrance of the original. This explains the connection between Mnemosyne and fame; the man who is surrounded by fame steps into the presence of the eternally valid. This explains also the connection between the Muses and the "view" in which, through the roots of every original science, we put the chaos in order with the aid of our founded knowledge.

Now we can begin to understand what Plato meant when he spoke of the condition of men before the birth of the Muses, in other words, what the Muses brought men and why those who devoted themselves to them forgot everything in favor of musical activities; the chaos was overcome, order was created, a cosmos appeared. We also must consider rhetoric from this aspect. On the basis of what we have just said, Plato cannot possibly identify true rhetoric with *episteme* which, due to its rational character, excludes all musical elements.

In the second part of the *Phaedrus* Plato attempts to clarify the nature of "true" rhetoric. He starts out with the demonstration that the process, which has its roots in the *nous* [*dia-noia*] as the insight into original "ideas," is the requisite for a true speech. The *dianoia* is the process which can be realized only on the basis of, or "through" [*dia*]—the *nous*. Socrates maintains that the orator must possess *dianoia* with respect to the subject he is talking about. *Dia-noia* is the faculty which leads us to a discernment through the *nous*, i.e., on the basis of an insight into the *archai*. *Nous* forms the prerequisite of *episteme* insofar as *episteme* can only prove or explain something following an insight [*noein*] into the original indicative, commanding, and showing images [*eide*]. The corresponding speech is neither purely rational nor purely pathetic.

Also it does not arise from a posterior unity which presupposes the duality of *ratio* and *passio,* but illuminates and influences the passions through its original, imaginative characters. Thus philosophy is not a posterior synthesis of *pathos* and *logos but the original unity* of the two under the power of the original *archai.* Plato sees true rhetoric as psychology which can fulfill its truly "moving" function only if it masters original images [*eide*]. Thus the true philosophy is rhetoric, and the true rhetoric is philosophy, a philosophy which does not need an "external" rhetoric to convince, and a rhetoric that does not need an "external" content of verity.

To sum up we are forced to distinguish between three kinds of speech: (1) The *external, "rhetorical speech,"* in the common meaning of this expression, which only refers to images because they affect the passions. Since these images do not stem from insight, however, they remain an object of opinion. This is the case of the purely emotive, false speech: "rhetoric" in the usual negative sense. (2) The *speech which arises exclusively from a rational proceeding.* It is true that this is of a demonstrative character, but it cannot have a rhetorical effect because purely rational arguments do not attain to the passions, i.e., "theoretical" speech in the usual sense. (3) The *true rhetorical speech.* This springs from the *archai,* nondeducible, moving, and indicative, due to its original images. The original speech is that of the wise man, of the *sophos,* who is not only *epistetai,* but who with insight leads, guides, and attracts.

The Metaphorical Basis of Rhetoric and Philosophy

I have attempted here to demonstrate that the problem of rhetoric in every sense cannot be separated from a discussion of its relation to philosophy. One problem, however, seems yet unsolved, namely, that an essential moment of rhetorical speech is metaphor. Can we claim that the original, archaic assertions on which rational proofs depend have a metaphorical character? Can we maintain the thesis that the *archai* have any connection with images as the subject of a "transferred" meaning? Surprisingly enough, perhaps, we can speak about first principles only through metaphors; we speak of them as "premises" [*premittere*], as "grounds," as "foundations," as "axioms" [*axiou* or estimate]. Even logical language must resort to metaphors, involving a transposition from the empirical realm of senses, in which "seeing" and the "pictorial" move to the foreground: to "clarify," to "gain insight," to "found," to "conclude," to "deduce." We also must not forget that the term "metaphor" is itself a metaphor; it is derived from the verb *metapherein* "to transfer," which originally described a concrete activity (Herodotus 1. 64.2).

Some authors limit the function of the metaphor to the transposition of words, i.e., of a word from its "own" field to another. Yet this transposition cannot be effected without an immediate insight into the *similarity* which appears in different fields. Aristotle says: "A good transposition is the sight of similar things." Thus this kind of "literary" metaphor already is based on the "discovery" of a *similar nature;* its function is to make visible a "common" quality between fields. It presupposes a "vision" of something hitherto concealed; it "shows" to the reader or to the spectator a common quality which is not rationally deducible.

But we must go a step deeper than the "literary" plane. The metaphor lies at the root of our human world. Insofar as metaphor has its roots in the analogy between different things and makes this analogy immediately spring into "sight," it makes a fundamental contribution to the structure of our world. Empirical observation itself takes place through the "reduction" of sensory phenomena to types of meanings existing in the living being; and this "reduction" consists in the "transferring" of a meaning to sensory phenomena. It is only through this "transference" that phenomena can be recognized as similar or dissimilar, useful or useless, for our human realization. In order to make "sensory" observations we are forced to "reach back" for a transposition, for a metaphor. Man can manifest himself only through his own "transpositions," and this is the essence of his work in every field of human activity.

On the theoretical level, types, which are based on the analogical process (i.e., reduction of multiplicity to unity on the basis of the *"transference" of a meaning* to the multiplicity), a process which when carried out culminates in philosophical knowledge, only can be expressed metaphorically in their nature and in their function. The metaphor lies at the root of our knowledge in which rhetoric and philosophy attain their original unity. Therefore we cannot speak of rhetoric *and* philosophy, but every original philosophy is rhetoric and every true and not exterior rhetoric is philosophy.

The metaphorical, pictorial nature of every original insight links insight with *pathos,* content with the form of speech. Thus the following words regarding effective instruction acquire a topical meaning:

> But if we regard speech with a view to its aim, it serves *to express, to teach, and to move [ad exprimendum, ad erudiendum, et ad movendum].* But it always expresses something by means *of an image [mediante specie],* it teaches by means *of a force of light [mediante lumine].* Now it is true that all this only happens through an *inner image, an inner light, and an inner force* that *are internally* connected with the soul *[quod non fit nisi per speciem et lumen et virtutem intrinsecam, intrinsecas animae unitas].*
>
> (Bonaventura, *Itinerarium mentis in Deum,* 18)

This is why the Middle Ages metaphorically saw nature, the environment of man and animal, as a book, as a transposition of the absolute *[conari debemus per speculum videre].* Philosophy itself becomes possible only on the basis of metaphors, on the basis of the ingenuity which supplies the foundation of every rational, derivative process.

Historical and Theoretical Premises of the Humanistic Conception of Rhetoric

Descartes and Vico

Descartes's Rationalistic Rejection of Humanistic Knowledge

Knowledge of the common basis of *pathos* and *logos*, stemming from the realization of the power of original images as the source of every true philosophy, was destroyed by modern rationalism.[1] As a result it also was forgotten that this very problem played an essential part in Italian Humanism. Whatever philosophical problems were discussed before Descartes, by the humanists and throughout the Renaissance, were regarded merely as more or less obscure "premonitions" of ideas that were clearly developed later by Descartes and subsequent modern thinkers. This attitude distinctly appears in Hegel's *History of Philosophy*[2] and is taken up later by the Italian followers of Hegel (Spaventa, Croce, Gentile). Subsequently it undergoes a change through the theory of Cassirer. He investigates Humanism and the Renaissance as to their philosophical significance, especially in regard to the problem of cognition, and evaluates the philosophy of that period above all only as a "premonition" of this problem.[3]

The general opinion in this connection is that the humanist tradition is primarily of literary and aesthetical significance rather than of philosophical significance. This view has its origin in statements of Descartes. Cartesian theories continue to determine even today's attitude toward the cultural ideal of Humanism and the supremacy of the word. Against Descartes's views I wish to explore the tradition of Italian Humanism that does not separate *res* from *verba*. These thinkers conceived philosophy as based on the faculty of *ingenium* and did not understand philosophical thought as something independent of rhetoric. By attention to Italian humanist thought I intend to show the priority of "topical" and "inventive" thinking over the critical and rational modes of thought that have dominated philosophy since Descartes.

Descartes examines and evaluates humanist branches of learning only with a view to determining whether and to what extent they are capable of providing truth and certainty in the sense of rational cognition. The authors of classical antiquity must be read, in his opinion, for the sake of rational knowledge, and so, for instance, a knowledge of ancient languages only serves to provide a rational understanding of classical texts. For Descartes, however, those studies that are handed down by tradition have lost altogether their philosophical significance. He believes that he can find more original minds outside the circles of the humanistic, literary tradition: "Often we see that those who have never concerned themselves with letters have by far a surer and clearer judgment about matters of everyday life than those who constantly remain in the schools."[4]

A critique of this kind is even more sharply formulated in the *Discours de la méthode*. Descartes believes that he can find more truth in the deliberations which each person makes about matters concerning himself, free from any literary and humanistic formation, than in those "which a scholar makes in his study about ineffective theories, which at most result in his becoming the more conceited, the more they are removed from common sense, since he has to use so much more wit and artifice in order to give them a semblance of truth."[5]

For Descartes the point of view represented by the first Italian humanists[6] remains incomprehensible, for instance, their thesis that philology in its original meaning is an essential element in the development of the human mind and, what is more, that it is in language that the nature of man reveals itself, so that the teaching of language may have a purpose and a sense of its own, as well as acquiring philosophical significance.

Similarly rhetoric—one of the fundamental branches of traditional humanistic culture—is, in his opinion, devoid of any positive meaning; whatever clever rules on beautiful speech it may give us, the best, if not the only, method to convince is the severity of logical proof, which leads to truth.[7]

Even references to classical antiquity seem unimportant to him; when concerning oneself with ancient authors, he explicitly says, one even runs the risk of having misconceptions establish themselves in the mind. "One has to read the books of ancient authors in order to find out what was correctly discovered in those days. . . . But now and then there is a great danger that the stains of error may adhere to us in our all-too attentive readings, however cautious we may be."[8] Thus Descartes sees in the humanist tradition merely a matter of scholarship, which is without any philosophical significance.

This entire attitude can be summed up in a single thesis: If the problem of philosophy is identical with that of rational knowledge, if this knowledge in its turn consists of tracing back our assertions to a "first truth," then emotive elements and with them the influence of images, of fantasy, of rhetoric play no role whatsoever in this rational process. They even appear as elements which interfere with the rational process.

So the consciousness of philosophical tradition is changed entirely. All classical authors quoted up to Descartes in philosophical treatises lose their significance as authorities, for the writers who had such a strong influence on humanist thought, such as Cicero, Quintilian, Lucian, and Lucretius, hardly could contribute to epistemological speculations. Here the theoretical depreciation of the philosophy of Humanism and the Renaissance begins, and basically continues until today, for the interest we are prepared to devote to the philosophy of that period is mainly historical.

Vico's Characterization of Descartes's Philosophy

At the end of the humanist period Vico—in whose theories the whole humanist tradition reached its highest philosophical consciousness—is in radical opposition to Descartes and tries to reestablish the connection between philosophy and rhetoric and, at the same time, to reinstate the humanistic branches of knowledge—which Descartes treated negatively and without comprehension—by rendering their philosophical significance. For this reason I will summarize briefly Vico's critique of Descartes's rationalistic philosophy.

In the third chapter of his *De studiorum ratione* (1709), Vico says that his contemporaries tried to establish new foundations for the building of science, mainly by starting out with a "*critical* attitude in philosophizing." His thesis is: "First of all, in what concerns the implements of science, we now begin our inquiries with the critique of cognition."[9] Vico here literally alludes to Descartes's claim that his philosophy is not dogmatic but "critical." This claim means that no thesis may be valid unless it is proved by a precise demonstration. As I have already mentioned, Descartes wants to surmount the philosophical tradition in which he was reared in order to find a new, unshakable foundation for philosophy, which is to lead out of the confusion of contradictions and dilemmas.

This, however, does not exhaust the claims of the "critical" method; Vico's next sentence informs us about it: "The critique intends to keep its *first truth*."[10] Philosophy and science hence acquire a distinctly *rational* character; if a first, nonderivable truth has been found, it is left to "critical" philosophy alone to draw any results from it through the rational process of conclusion and deduction.

Should a single first truth be considered as the foundation for philosophy, all other truths would be degraded to "second truths" [*vera secunda*]. *Vera secunda* are those truths that form the foundations for individual sciences. The axioms of mathematics are valid solely for being *as* number; those of geometry for being *as* size; and those of physics for being *as* movement. The *vera secunda* consequently are valid only with regard to being *as* this or *as* that. They also can be replaced by other fundamental truths or axioms; depending on what principles are at the basis one can speak, for instance, of a three-dimensional, Euclidian, or other geometry. The same is true of mathematics, of physics, etc. The sphere of the *vera secunda* corresponds to that of the classical *techne*; the individual sciences are *technai* which, on the basis of certain premises, attain individual cognition. We will not go into the question of what criteria determine the choice of the principles for each individual science. We could prove that the individual sciences in reality are not ruled by theoretical or epistemological laws because they are concerned primarily with mastering nature. Already the ancient *technai* were of a "mechanical" nature (in the sense of *mechane* "expedients"), for their aim was to produce something of service to mankind.

According to Descartes the individual sciences, if they are to be strictly scientific, should be derived from "first truths," and hence possess a philosophical character which transcends the barriers separating them. This very conception had a decisive influence on the subsequent evolution of modern thought insofar as it goes back to Descartes and has survived particularly in German Idealism. From Fichte to Hegel, German Idealism strives to derive individual sciences rigorously from philosophi-

cal premises and principles in order to erect a systematic structure of sciences. This enterprise leads to the idealistic effort of
achieving a priori derivation of the structure of natural sciences;
Hegel, in this sense, went to the ultimate conclusion, which in
its turn brought about the anti-idealistic and anti-philosophical
reaction of the second half of the nineteenth century.

Incidentally, these attempts to anchor natural sciences in a
"first truth" and to give them a philosophical foundation in
order to build a complete system of sciences are diametrically
opposed to the humanistic tradition beginning with Leonardo
da Vinci and culminating in the theories of Galileo. In this
tradition the natural sciences are interpreted exclusively with
regard to their practical, purposeful performances, and are
exempted completely from epistemological functions. From this
point of view, for instance, nature remains unknown to
Leonardo; that is, it reveals itself each time only within the
limits of those questions which man asks in the framework of an
experiment.

Vico's Affirmation of the Sphere of Pure Possibilities

According to Vico, Descartes not only rejects every "second
truth," but also every probability [*verisimilia*]. In order to
understand Vico's term *verisimile*, we have to go back to ancient
philosophy. Aristotle maintains that knowledge can exist only
of something which occurs regularly and of necessity, for
knowledge means to grasp the grounds of a conformity. Whatever manifests itself differently, i.e., whatever changes, cannot
be an object of knowledge. These phenomena include, in particular, human actions and attitudes because they constantly are
faced with different situations to which man is forced to react
differently each time. In this field, according to Aristotle's
Rhetoric, the determining factor is not rationally deducible
truth, but probability.

If Descartes's main aspirations are directed toward a "first
truth," it follows necessarily that the sphere of pure possibilities, and with it the sphere of "probability," is excluded
from philosophy. Thus Descartes ignores, for example, both the
art of rhetoric and history, as fields in which "the probable,"
rather than the truth, prevails. Vico speaks of the significance of
"probability" as follows: "From the probable, there arises
natural common sense, which is the norm of all practical intelligence [*prudentiae*] and hence also of eloquence. For orators
have more difficulty with a true state of affairs which does not

seem probable than with a false one making a plausible impression."[11]

Vico attaches importance to pointing out the negative results of critical philosophy by showing what fields it excludes from the realm of philosophical formation. He enumerates them (poetry, rhetoric, political education, history), and designates the *verisimile* as the common ground in which they have their roots, the probable which is not determined by the true nor by the knowledge it engenders. The art of eloquence belongs to the realm of probability because it constantly directs its glance at the specific, variable psychic state of the audience; similarly practical intelligence belongs to this realm—*prudentia*, the specific political ability—because it concerns itself with the constantly variable individual case.

The defects of rationalistic, critical philosophy are much more important than they appear at first sight. By failing to take into account political faculties and the art of eloquence, this philosophy disregards two of the most important branches of human activity. The one-sided concern about truth misses the preparation for recognizing individual cases, and it ignores the necessity for political education.

Vico formulates this idea clearly in *De studiorum ratione:* "But this order of studies brings with it the disadvantage for young people, that in the future they will neither show intelligence in civil life [*nec satis vitam civilem prudenter agant*], nor be able to enliven a speech with characteristic colours [*nec orationem moribus tingere*] and warm it with the fire of emotions."[12]

Vico proceeds with his objections by stressing that Descartes's rationalistic, critical method not only neglects decisive fields of human activity but also ignores the nature and role of the image, and with it, of fantasy, in favor of the rational.

> Finally, they [our critics] set their *first truth* above every image of the body [*Denique ante, extra super omnes . . . suum primum elocant verum*]. . . . Now as old age brings reason [*ratio*] to bloom, so youth does with fantasy. . . . And memory which, if not directly identical with fantasy, is closely related to it, has to be developed in children because they have no other mental faculty; nor ought one to suppress abilities for the arts [*neque ingenia ad artes*], which consist of fantasy and memory or a combination of both, as for example paint-

ing, poetry, rhetoric and jurisprudence [*neque . . . sunt hebetanda*].[13]

Topical and Rational Philosophy

The Classical Conception of Topics

The terminology that Vico uses in his polemics against Rationalism strikes us, as well as most historians of philosophy, as odd; in most instances it is considered merely as a reference to a dated and dusty set of problems. Vico's polemics against Descartes are carried out in the framework of the terminological distinction between "critical" and "topical" or "inventive" philosophy.

Between *inventio* and "topics" on one side and "critical philosophy" on the other, the following connection seems to result. After "discovering" a first truth on which to build a system of sciences, *the entire scientific process necessarily consists of a strictly rational deduction.* Nevertheless the thesis that philosophy must restrict itself to this process is untenable, according to Vico, mainly because deduction presupposes another activity, the very activity of "finding." Vico claims that the aim of philosophy is the problem of "finding," and he identifies the theory of "finding" with "topical philosophy." The problem of finding, as present in the Cartesian theory of *clarté* and "distinction" as the "sight" of a primary and universal truth, is insufficient because it does not resolve the problem of grasping the concrete situation. The possibilities and the aim of rhetorical speech are the following: "For as the discovery of general arguments is by nature *prior to the judgement* about their truth [*Nam ut argumentorum inventio prior natura est, quam de eorum veritate diiudicatio*], so the teaching of *topics* must be prior to that of criticism [*ita topica prior critica debet esse doctrina*]."[14]

Before proceeding to a closer examination of the philosophical significance which Vico attaches to "topical philosophy," we should bear in mind what was meant by this term in classical antiquity. The first sentence of Aristotle's *Topics* does not appear to apply to nor to clarify the connection Vico sees between topics and philosophy. "The aim of this treatise consists of finding a method with which to form, with regard to every proposed examination, syllogisms that are derived from elements *based on opinion* [*ek endoxon*], so that we may say nothing that contradicts the thesis we ourselves presented."[15] Aristotle goes on to distinguish the syllogisms resulting from original premises from those based on opinions. This differentiation makes it possible for him to rationalize the usefulness of topics. For if the opinions of the majority are known, and if one has a method for finding the required arguments quickly, it will be much easier to dispute with the opponent; in view of the sciences connected with philosophy, topics finally make it possible to recognize the difficulties of a problem when it can be solved in one way or another.[16] In fact topics, according to an example given by Aristotle, supply that which also is necessary in dialectic; all arguments must be "at hand" in order to be used at the right moment.

The function of topics is to determine "how many and what kinds of arguments the speech requires, and what elements they consist of, and how easily we can find the speeches."[17]

Aristotle's theses which we have quoted here enable us to guess how Vico succeeds in ascribing philosophical significance to topics. The Aristotelian theory of topics concerns the "finding" of arguments that are needed for a rhetorical speech. Even the first principles, as we know, cannot be "proved" rationally, they can only be "found." So we come up against the question of whether Vico perhaps saw a connection between topics and philosophy from this aspect.

To answer this question I will refer to statements by Cicero and Quintilian. Cicero says in his *De oratore:* "But Aristotle, for whom I have the highest admiration, has set up certain *loci* [*posuit quosdam locos*], departing from which one cannot only discover every method for an argument in philosophical discussions [*ex quibus omnis argumenti via non modo ad philosophorum disputationem*], but which also can be used in all legal cases."[18]

We must be aware of the fact that the Greek word *topoi* is translated here by the Latin term *loci.* In other passages Cicero also uses, among other expressions, the words *sedes argumentorum.* Similarly Tacitus says in his dialogue about orators: "We take over from the peripatetics the places that are useful and ready for every discussion [*in omnem disputationem paratos iam locos*]."[19]

For a successful discussion all arguments have to be at hand. In other words one must know the *loci,* the places where they are to be found easily. Here, too, topics would mean the theory of arguments or points of departure which have to be available in a concrete situation for a discussion, whether of a logical or a rhetorical kind.

The Problem of "Invention"

In the following quotations from Cicero's *Topics*, the term *locus* is followed by a verb which is very important in connection with our question: *invenire.*

> Just as of those things that are concealed, the proof and the *discovery* are easy if the place is noted and indicated [*demonstrato et notato loco facilis inventio est*], so if we examine a theme, we must know its place; thus they are called by Aristotle places, as it were, from which the arguments stem, and so one can say that the place is the seat of arguments [*locum esse argumenti sedem*].[20]

In order to explain Vico's questions and terminology, another important statement by Cicero should be mentioned, which is obviously the source of Vico's differentiation between topical and critical philosophy. Cicero consciously distinguishes between inventive and derivative, i.e., rational activity, which he describes as dialectic.

> Every careful method consists of two parts: one of *inventing* and one of *judging* [*omnis ratio diligens disserendi duas habeat partes, unam inveniendi, alteram iudicandi*]. The Stoics have developed with great diligence the ways of *judging,* and that by means of the science they call dialectic; the *art of inventing,* which is called topic[s] . . . they have completely neglected [*inveniendi artem, quae "topike" dicitur . . . totam reliquerunt*].[21]

Here "topics" and "dialectic" are facing one another; it is for dialectic to draw *conclusions* by means of rational deduction, while topics represent the art of *invention,* just as it was seen in the Middle Ages, for example, by Boethius, who, in his treatise *De differentiis topicis,* stresses the *inventive* nature of topics insofar as they serve the process to *trahere argumenta.*[22]

In this context we might recall the traditional division of the art of rhetoric. Above all, *matter* and *form* of speech, i.e., *what* is said and *how* it is said, are distinguished. "Every speech consists of that which is designated and that which designates, i.e., of *things* and *words.*" Each single political, legal, or panegyric speech consists of five elements: among them, the *inventio* takes the first place. "The entire capacity of the orator is divided into five parts, namely first he must find what he wants to say, then he must put together what he has found not only in the right order, but also with a certain weight and with judgment."[23] Whether one wants to carry out a rational process or try to make rhetorical deductions, one always has to "find" the premises first; it is the *inventio* which supplies the arguments to make an effective rational or rhetorical speech possible. In the system of rhetoric the *inventio* and the *dispositio* concern the subject *matter;* the *elocutio* or the *vestire* and *ornare* refer to the *form;* the *actio* finally brings about the union of matter and form, of *res* and *verba.*

The Prevalence of "Topical," "Inventive" as Opposed to "Critical," Rational Philosophy

In his *De studiorum ratione* Vico complains that modern authors despise topics and are convinced, as a result of their exclusive concentration on method, that it is sufficient to be informed about a matter to *find* immediately what is true in it [*"nam sat est, inquiunt, . . . rem doceri, ut quid in ea veri inest inveniant"*].[24] Correspondingly, says Vico, the rationalists claim to be able to derive the "probable," which borders on truth, on the basis of logical rules. But "finding" here is identified with the process of deduction going back to a first truth, and is simply interpreted in a *rational* sense.

The problem which concerns Vico as to the philosophical significance of topics lies, however, in an entirely different direction; it centers on the question of whether the rational process is adequate as a key to phenomena. The original "finding," the *invenire,* never can occur within a deductive process because it cannot reach beyond its premises. Vico's rejection of the critical method, and of the Rationalism connected with it, is based on the recognition that the original premises as such are nondeducible and that the *rational process* hence cannot "find" them; that, moreover, rational knowledge cannot be a determining factor for rhetorical or poetic speech because it cannot comprehend the particular, the individual, i.e., the concrete situation; and since the critical method always starts with a premise, its final conclusions are necessarily valid only generally.

> Topics is the theory of original vision, which is the source of "ingenious," i.e., rationally non-deducible

forms of teaching and learning. Topics *finds* and *collects* [*ritruova ed ammassa*]; critique divides and analyses what has been collected [*la critica dall'ammassato divide e rimuove*]; that is why topical minds are richer and less true [*più copiosi e men veri*], while critical minds are truer but drier [. . . *più veri, ma però asciutti*].[25]

Ingenium as the Basis of Topical Speech

Vico repeatedly defends topics against the prevalence of rational activity on the grounds that the premises from which conclusions are drawn have to be "perceived" to begin with. This perception is the function of topics because, and here the new important term appears, they come from the *ingenium* and not from the *ratio*.

> Providence has well arranged human things by awakening in the human mind first topics, and then critique, just as the cognition of things precedes judgment about them [*siccome prima è conoscere, poi giudicar delle cose*]. For topic is the faculty which makes minds "ingenious" [*la topica è la facultà di far le menti ingegnose*], just as critique makes them precise [*la critica è di farle esatte*]; and in early times the question was, above all, to find those things that are necessary for human life, and finding is the property of *ingenium* [*e il ritruovare è proprietà dell' ingegno*].[26]

Ingenium is the source of the creative activity of topics. "The special faculty of knowing lies in the *ingenium*, with its help man *collects* the things *which to those who possess no ingenium seem to be without any relationship to one another* [*compone le cose, le quali, a coloro che pregio d'ingegno non hanno, sembravano non aver tra loro nessun rapporto*]." *Ingenium* is the "grasping" [*comprensiva*], rather than the "deductive" property. The grasp, however, precedes the deduction because we can draw conclusions only from what we have already grasped. "*Ingenium* is the faculty to unite what is dispersed and diverse."[27]

To the idea just developed we may add the following remark. The difference between critical and topical philosophy, as worked out by Vico, is by no means a dated, but a very current, problem. Today we are proud, for example, of the science of cybernetics and we rely on it for the future of the human community, but we forget that for it, too, the main problem is finding the points of departure, for the cybernetic process can only work on and draw its conclusions from elements already "found." The necessary achievement of human *ingenium* cannot be reduced to purely rational, derivative processes, as they are practiced today to an incommensurable degree by logistics.

Quintilian as the Source of Humanistic Awareness of the Union of *res* and *verba*

The Problem

Vico's theories on topical philosophy are rooted in the Latin humanist tradition, in a tradition which ascribes a chief role to rhetoric. The humanist tradition always has concerned itself with the union of *res* and *verba*, of *"content"* and *"form,"* with those elements of human speech that, once separated, cannot be reunited. If one accepts exclusively the rational element in a speech, that is, the prevalence of the *rational content*, then it will be possible to give the speech merely an *"external," rhetorical "form."*

Our reference to Descartes has shown how the priority he gives to rational knowledge channels the quest for the unconcealed into a decidedly rationalistic direction. From the very beginning he strips the humanistic branches of their philosophical significance. Vico's critique of Cartesian thought and his differentiation between critical and topical philosophy are all the more important because they show that the identification of unconcealment with rational knowledge covers up all those fields in which either fantasy (as in rhetoric, or in poetry), or *prudentia* (as in political ability) are determining factors. This is the reason why Vico appeals against the one-sidedness of a purely critical, rationalistic formation. Vico has herewith provided us with a new, often neglected, access to the entire approach of Humanism, to which we must now turn our attention, in order to show the prevalence of the image, which also comes out in this historical perspective.

Vico, by identifying the original source of philosophy with the inventional element of topics, which forms a decisive part of rhetoric, unexpectedly leads not only philosophy and rhetoric to a renewed union (so compelling that, as Vico expresses it, philosophy has to have a topical character), but also proves the union of *pathos* with ingenious, originating insight.

Therein with the humanistic tradition we come up against the problem of uniting rhetorical and philosophical speech. As *pathos* is the element through which the content of a speech achieves its effect, and as *pathos* itself is moved through images, it is clear that in the rationalistic tradition the emotive is identified with the "formal" aspect of speech and the element of insight with the "content," with the subject matter. Long since in antiquity the problem of the connection between *pathos* and insight appears as that of "form" and "content" of a speech, and Cicero in *De oratore* already deplores the loss of the union of these two.

What is at the root of the humanistic tradition of the union of *res* and *verba*, "content" and "form?" In connection with antiquity we will restrict ourselves to pointing out how the problem of the union of content and form of speech was conceived by Quintilian, who, like Cicero, had a decisive influence on the humanist tradition.

Quintilian's Thesis: Nothing Is Alien to the Art of Speech

Quintilian's *Institutiones oratoriae* represents one of the classical texts of rhetoric; it is the end result of Ciceronian theories. In accordance with rhetorical tradition Quintilian considers every speech as consisting of five elements: one is the content, *res,* which has its origin in the *inventio,* while the other four elements belong to the form, the *verba*. "Every method of speech consists of five parts: invention, arrangement, linguistic form, memory, delivery or presentation."[28] It is not sufficient to "find" *what,* under the respective circumstances, "must" be said, but *how,* whereby memory and the method of delivery must correspond to the concrete historical situation in which the orator finds himself. Quintilian, following the Aristotelian analysis, distinguishes three kinds of speech: the legal, the political, and the eulogistic. The reason for this division of the rhetorical art has been mentioned already; the temporal structure of the human world, the world *which is not, but "becomes,"* forces us to form the speech with a view to the future or to the past or to that which is valid and, therefore, praiseworthy.

Earlier, in the introduction to the *Institutiones oratoriae,* a thesis is expressed which is important in connection with our problem: most people, says Quintilian, approach the art of rhetoric as though they were already conversant with all other realms of knowledge, and as though they were lacking in nothing but eloquence. *"Nam ceteri fere qui artem orandi litteris tradiderunt, ita sunt exorsi, quasi perfectis omni alio genere doctrinae summam in eloquentiae manum imponerent."*[29] According to this conception rhetoric would be a kind of "formal" supplement to the "content" or "subject matter" attained through science. Here the dualism appears between rhetorical form and scientific rational content, where rhetoric is to assume merely the function of an "external activation" to lend effect to the rational content.

To this conception Quintilian opposes a thesis of his own, which at first surprises us: *Nothing* is alien to the art of speech, for *any content* of speech has its *own rhetorical* form. *"Ego quum existimem nihil arti oratoriae alienum, sine quo fieri non posse oratorem fatendum est."*[30] Is Quintilian's thesis to be interpreted to mean—as Cicero's in *De oratore*—that the orator, since *no* field ought to be alien to him, should master all branches of knowledge? A requirement of this kind is unintelligible to us, for it borders on Utopia. Here we find one of the causes for our present negative judgment about the claims of traditional rhetoric.

Rhetoric concerns the emotive speech, science the rational speech. If Quintilian considers rhetoric as appropriate for every kind of speech, he must abolish the duality of "matter" and "form." So he emphasizes that "originally" the separation between the two elements of speech *did not* exist: "These [content and form, wisdom and eloquence] were, as Cicero already proves, *just as they were unified by nature,* so also connected in practice, whereby *the same men were esteemed as wise and eloquent."*[31]

This union, says Quintilian, was lost later [*scidit deinde se studium*], probably as a result of indolence, which also soon led the orators to neglect their concern for morality [*curam morum . . . reliquerunt*] and, on the other hand, because only scholars claimed for themselves the appellation "Explorers of Wisdom" [*ut soli studiosi sapientiae vocarentur*].[32]

For Quintilian, however, *res* and *verba* are the original constituents of *every* meaningful utterance: "Every utterance through which someone manifests a will necessarily has content and word." The subject matter of rhetoric hence consists of *whatever is an object of speech;* it is found in the three types of speech already mentioned: the eulogistic, the advisory, and the legal.[33]

The Fundamental Union of *res* and *verba* Grounded in the
Specific Situation of Man

The fundamental theory about the union of content and form of
speech particularly requires, in our opinion, a clearer explanation of an often neglected exposition by Quintilian about the
subject matter of the legal speech, which acquires special
significance in connection with surmounting the dualism between content and form. By way of introduction Quintilian
again refers to his basic thesis that *everything can be the subject
matter* of rhetoric. The premise of a legal debate is found,
according to Quintilian, in the *status* of things, understood as a
conflicting situation out of which the *causa*, the "case," arises.
On closer observation, however, it appears that it is not only the
status, i.e., the case which "stands" before us, that forms the
real subject matter of the legal speech, but the problem contained in it, which affects the lawyer. At the bottom of each
debate there lies a state [*status*] of the matter ["*Ergo quum omnis
causa contineatur aliquo statu*"]. What we call status, some call
statement, others *questioning*:

> [*id quidam constitutionem vocant, alii quaestionem (voc-
> ant)*]. . . . Some say that the *state* of the matter is the first
> *conflict of legal matters* [*statum quidam dixerunt primam
> causarum conflictionem*]; they have, I believe, sensed the
> right thing, but expressed themselves inadequately. *It is
> not the first conflict*—as, for instance, you have done it, I
> have not done it [*non enim est status prima conflictio:
> fecisti, non feci*]—, but what comes out of the first
> conflict, namely the *kind of question* [*sed quod ex prima
> conflictione nascitur, id est genus quaestionis*].[34]

The subject matter of the legal speech, therefore, does not
exhaust itself in the existing state of affairs, for it is supplied by
the *legal problem* which contains it and which only the "capable" lawyer can discover. The legal "matter" hence does not
consist of a mute "existing" state of affairs, but of the *entire
questionableness* of the respective case.[35]

Further on in his argument Quintilian refers to Aristotle's
analysis of the different categories of being, with the help of
which one can question phenomena. For the Greeks the questioning of a phenomenon as to its being, its quality, and its
quantity meant to "accuse," i.e., to define being as one thing or
another. Quintilian traces back the Greek term *categoria* to this

original meaning, and also as regards legal matters.[36] Now if the specific situation of man consists of his having to define all that is, i.e., of having to "accuse" it in terms of categories, in order to set up a human order, then being can appear only as *quaestio*, and we can respond to it only as to something of concern to us. In the same manner the subject matter of the legal speech dissolves in the multiplicity of those questions which concern the human being there, and on the basis of which the phenomenon can be delimited and defined, i.e., can assume a recognizable shape.

The theory of categories applies to every kind of speech:

> There are three questions which come up in every discussion: whether something is, what it is, how it is: *what even nature itself prescribes for us [an sit, quid sit, quale sit: quod ipsa nobis etiam natura praescribit]*. For *first an object of conflict must exist [Nam primum oportet subesse aliquid, de quo ambigitur]*. . . . Here is the ground for indefinite or definite questions. From here, in any case, one thing or another is dealt with in ostentatious, counselling, legal eloquence *[His infinitae quaestiones, his finitae continentur. Horum aliqua in demonstrativa, deliberativa, judiciali materia utique tractatur]*.[37]

The problems of rhetoric hereby apply not merely to a special sphere of human existence but to every human activity and method of action. This makes it clear that Quintilian attributes to the subject matter of rhetoric an essential, existential significance insofar as this subject matter—always within the three perspectives of future, present, and past, corresponding to the political, eulogistic, or legal speech—appears as *quaestio* which concerns the human being. "By question in the wider sense, there is to be understood everything that can be spoken of in a creditable manner in two opposite or several directions."[38]

The Close Link between *nomina* and *verba*

Quintilian also discusses the intimate link between subject matter and form, between content and shape of speech, by means of another very important argument. Grammar, says Quintilian, consists of two main elements: the teaching of correct speech, which includes the teaching of spelling, and the interpretation of poets, which is done with the help of criticism.[39] Grammar, insofar as it examines the various parts of speech, proves that res *[materia, nomina]* and *vis sermonis* [*verba*] are inseparable, since no speech can be constructed exclusively from *verba* or from *nomina*. In the verb the force of the speech is concentrated [*in verbis vim sermonis*], and in the noun the subject matter [*in nominibus materiam*]. The verb makes a statement about the relationship toward that which is not yet, no longer, or now, so that it evokes such feelings as hope, anxiety, and longing. Men and things, on the other hand, are evoked by nouns. From the grammatical point of view the union of *res* and *verba* consists of the close link between object and verb, which can express the emotion. Referring to antiquity, Quintilian says: "For they believed that the verbs contained the force of the speech, the nouns the subject matter (for one is that which we say, the other that of which we say something), and the conjunctions their compilation." His thesis that every matter can be experienced only in a temporal and hence emotive sense, and, therefore, cannot be separated from the verb, is substantiated by a quotation from Horace: "Provide the subject, and the words will follow on their own."[40]

The "subject matter" of rhetoric hence results from the insight into all that which concerns man in ever new "forms," and which, for that reason, has to be expressed; this insight itself is of the nature of an *inventio,* which places it, as the realization of human *ingenium,* at the source of original insight. This is why Quintilian advocates that the young should be provided with a rich diversity in subject matter for speech, for this alone gives rise to questions and helps the "inventive" spirit to develop. In Quintilian's expositions there appears a note of melancholy when he discovers that toward the decline of life, the *ratio* sneaks in gradually, choking up the insight into the original. With its peculiar characteristic of never being "at hand," but always having to be "discovered," the subject matter of speech confirms its "inventive" nature. This thesis was revived and developed by Humanism and during the Renaissance, especially in the field of politics. Machiavelli and Guicciardini maintain that political ability manifests itself mainly through someone being able to "find" the appropriate subject.[41] An abstract subject never will lead to political action, but only that subject which is "found" in the concrete historical situation.

This theory of the fundamental union of *res* and *verba* supplies the Italian humanists with, among other things, the reason why they wish to be "grammarians" rather than "philosophers." A philosopher is one who strives to make an exclusively rational speech without any access to the passions and who, therefore, stops at the gap between *res* and *verba*. The rhetorical formation represented programmatically by the humanists, on the contrary, aspires to a union of subject matter and word in the sense I have just developed.

The Humanistic Tradition: The Preeminence of Image and Indicative Speech on Rational Language

Poliziano as *Grammaticus*

In order to elucidate the manner in which our problem appears in the humanist tradition, we will, as an example, indicate a few statements by Poliziano. Like Petrarch, and subsequently Leonardo Bruni, he dedicated himself to the study of ancient texts; what primarily concerned him, and here he followed Petrarch and Salutati, was to save these texts materially from disappearing and to rescue them from oblivion, so that they could be available for interpretation. Concerning their material preservation, Poliziano writes:

> What use is it now to recall the misfortunes of times past? What we can hardly do reverently enough, without the greatest suffering, when those splendid authors, worthy of immortality, were partly disfigured and shamefully torn by the Barbarians, partly, as it were, thrown into the dungeon and held in fetters by them, until they at last, maimed and mangled and terribly altered, returned again to their fatherland.[42]

He is an "interpreter," a grammarian and not a philosopher, Poliziano protests at his inaugural lecture of 1492, which is entitled "Lamia." Here he deals with the question of what characteristics qualify him to interpret philosophical texts at his lessons at the *Studio fiorentino*. Poliziano asserts that during his lifetime the meaning of the word *grammaticus* has narrowed down considerably, for originally it was not the language teacher who was thus called, but the interpreter of texts, i.e., the person who, over and above the understanding of individual words and their correlations, was able to lead to a pertinent discussion of the content of a text.

> With the ancients this position [of *grammaticus*] was so highly esteemed that the grammarians were all censors and experts about the whole of literature [*apud antiquos olim tantum auctoritatis his ordo habuit, ut censores es-*

sent, et iudices scriptorum omnium soli grammatici]. The function of the grammarian is to examine and explain *every kind* of literature—the works of poets, historians, orators, philosophers, physicians, lawyers [*Grammaticorum enim sunt hae partes, ut omne scriptorum genus . . . enarrent*][43]

Now the question arises whether there is not a contradiction in Poliziano's statement insofar as he aspires at a comprehension of philosophical texts, although he wants to be a *grammaticus* rather than a philosopher. First of all, we should be aware of the fact that Poliziano by no means rejects philosophy; on the contrary the entire lecture "Lamia" is a defense of philosophy. "In a purified light we behold man and God. For if we fail to follow philosophy as a guide to life on the whole and to the exploration of virtue, and as the persecutor of vice . . . we shall never be able to shine in the pure light."[44]

Despite, or perhaps because of, his high esteem for philosophy, Poliziano insists on being a grammarian, for he is convinced that in his time the pressing task is to study philosophy with the aid of the ancient word rather than through theoretical speculation.

Poliziano confirms that his interpretation of the word, and so his task as a grammarian, is by no means identical with the teaching of language first of all by his assertion that his work is dependent not on the *ratio* but on the Muses. "Thus none shall praise what he has learnt, but put it concretely on the table before all. That I have, no doubt, done so far, with the acclaim of the Muses, to whom I consecrate myself, stricken with tremendous love."[45]

The attitude we have just outlined is confirmed by Poliziano further through his statement that he chooses those texts for interpretation that are so rich in questions as to be avoided for that very reason by most philosophers. "Even if the works have many thorns and abound in factual or conceptual difficulties [he refers to the *Analytica*], I will nevertheless tackle them with all the more preference, cheerfulness and enthusiasm, for they are omitted in almost all the philosophical schools of our days, not because they are considered useless, but because they are full of questions."[46] Finally he is fully conscious when tying up his own love for fables with the philosophical role of myths; they arouse astonishment and incite people to philosophize.

The Preeminence of Emotive Speech as Origin of Community

To question the words about their sense within the limits of a text—about a sense which a purely grammatical and lexical knowledge does not provide, for otherwise any person knowing a language could immediately understand the poets, the philosophers, the orators, and hence get to the heart of the "matter"—that is the way to philosophize, as acknowledged by Poliziano. In a polemical attitude against abstract philosophers, whom he describes as owls, he says at the end of the "Lamia": "For the old owls were indeed wise, now there are many owls that do have feathers, eyes and bills of owls, but do not have the wisdom."

Poliziano's claim that the *grammaticus,* as a connoisseur of the word, the expression, and the "form," also must have the faculty to interpret the "content," the "subject matter," and hence to preserve the original union of word (expression, form) and subject matter (content), owes its theoretical background to Quintilian. We referred earlier to those of Quintilian's statements in which he maintains that the subject matter always occurs and concerns us in the form of a question, that the noun is the expression of the subject matter and the verb the expression of the "form" in which the "subject matter" concerns us; that, therefore, there is no speech without the union of noun and verb. So it is already in the human language as such that the indissoluble union of content and form appears, the union which the grammarian above all, who starts out with language, attains so that he may claim to realize the original "comprehensive" philosophy.[47]

Following up Quintilian's theses Poliziano delivers an inaugural lecture about his *Institutiones* and about Statius's *Silvae,* in which he points out that the emotive speech represents the origin of every human content [res], because it is only through it that men have been able to form a community, which allows them to accede to their very own res. The study of the emotive speech hence boils down to the study of that which concerns man and guides his self-realization. "This matter alone (rhetoric) has united men, who had first been dispersed, to form a community, has reconciled those who fought against one another, and has bound them through laws, customs, and every human or civic culture."[48]

Rhetorical language is the ground of historicity of man who develops himself in the society. It promotes that which is useful to the state and, last though not least, causes the kind of speech to thrive which "polished with wit and urbanity, has nothing coarse, nothing inappropriate or uncultivated, but is spiced with all its politeness, all its seriousness and all its sweetness."[49]

There is an allusion here to what Guazzo later calls the *"conversazione civile,"* which is not merely "ornament" but constitutes the essence of human life. But what is the philosophical signification of rhetoric, imaginative, metaphoric speech?

Giovanni Pico's Letter *"De genere dicendi philosophorum,"* the Problem

In Italian Humanism and in the Renaissance the problem of the dualism of content and form, of *logos* and *pathos,* and simultaneously the attempt to eliminate this dualism, crops up again and again under new aspects. It would demand a voluminous study if scholars were to make an exhaustive compilation of such works. We are forced to restrict ourselves here to a few typical examples.

The crucial role played in the humanistic tradition by the problem we have in mind comes out, for instance, in the little treatise *De genere dicendi philosophorum,* by Giovanni Pico della Mirandola. The author does not stop at the problem of dualism between *res* and *verba* by contenting himself with the assertion that rhetorical speech cannot be replaced by rational speech; that is, he designs a solution of his own which deserves our attention.

The treatise is in fact a letter which Giovanni Pico della Mirandola sent to Hermolao Barbaro on June 3, 1485. Hermolao Barbaro himself, in a letter to Pico dated April 5, 1485, had criticized and rejected the style of scholastic philosophers, and of philosophers in general.[50] Because of this attitude Barbaro became known as the advocate of the "form" of literary, emotive speeches, while Giovanni Pico, due to the way in which his reply was interpreted, was considered as the advocate of the philosophical style, that is, of the *res* rather than the *verba*.

Before quoting and interpreting excerpts from Pico's letter, we should note that we interpret it in a sense which runs counter to the traditional view. E. Garin, for instance, maintains that Pico did not succeed in establishing the union of *res* and *verba* because in his antithesis to Barbaro he laid the stress on *res*. We are convinced, however, that Pico's letter is so significant because it achieves a theoretically unequivocal union of *res* and *verba* and discloses the difference between *rational* philosophy and primary topical philosophical insight. Barbaro emphasizes the claims of the *verba* in his letter.

> Of course, I do not count among Latin authors the Germanic and Teutonic ones, who did not really live during their own lifetime, much less so now that they are dead. . . . I do not completely refuse them everything that can be refused, but it is *brilliant and elegant* speech, or at least *clear and pure* speech [*sermo nitidus et elegans, saltem parus et castus*] . . . which brings fame and eternal remembrance to the writer [*laudem et memoriam sempiternam scriptoribus conciliat*].[51]

The argument Barbaro puts forward is: Should a thesis about the prevalence of "form" be rejected, then this would imply that a speech is to be praised because of its "matter" and that, by analogy, in the realm of art a work is praiseworthy only because of its "precious matter."[52]

Pico's Departure from the Prevalence of the Rational Speech

Pico begins his reply with a kind of prolegomenon in which he expresses his admiration for Barbaro. He then goes on to develop his thesis about the prevalence of philosophy as opposed to purely literary or philosophical enterprises or speeches. His words sound polemical: "Illustriously we have lived, oh Hermolao, and will live in [the] future, *not in the schools of grammarians and pedagogues,* but in the circle of philosophers and in the assembly of the wise, where there will be mention neither of the mother of Andromache, nor of the children of Niobe, nor of similar nonentities, but *of the principles* of things human and divine."[53]

Pico gives the following reasons for his conception: *(a)* The philosophers dispose of an internal rather than an external eloquence [*"habuisse barbaros non in lingua sed in pectore Mercurium"*]; *(b)* wisdom and eloquence are different in nature, the attempt to unite them is no less than sacrilegious [*"ut coniunxisse sit nefas"*]; *(c)* one can imagine no greater contrast than that between the functions of the orator and the philosopher [*"tanta est inter oratoris munus ac philosophi pugnantia, ut pugnare magis invicem non possint"*].[54] As the aim of rhetoric is evidently to deceive, philosophers would lose their authority were they to avail themselves of these emotive, seductive means. These are partially the same arguments that

Descartes—starting out with the prevalence of the *ratio*—was to direct against rhetoric. However, we shall see how Pico, owing to the fact that he does not take his departure from the prevalence of the *ratio,* reaches conclusions that are different from those of Descartes, namely, the recognition of an original speech which is philosophical as well as emotive or rhetorical, as opposed to the purely dialectic, scholastic, rational conception of philosophy, which it is his aim to surmount.

In Pico's letter there follows the defense of the primacy of the philosophical speech: It is distinguished by its unrhetorical character because it is not addressed to the senses; besides, any external ornament would destroy its unity.[55] Further Pico rejects Barbaro's criticism that scholastic philosophy uses bad rather than classical Latin. His argument is as follows: Classical Latin (Roman) language cannot be considered as the one and only valid prototype of a perfect language, for each period has its own style, not to speak of the fact that philosophers cannot waste their time on grammatical and lexical matters. In the last part of his letter, Pico once more stresses the prevalence of the content as the prevalence of philosophy.

When surveying the content of Pico's letter, we notice that the problem of the interrelation between content and form of speech is at the center; at the same time the traditional interpretation of this text—rejection of rhetoric and prevalence of philosophy over grammatical interests—appears as justified. Pico thinks that the lack of rhetorical ability with which the so-called barbarian philosophers have been reproached is no real sin because those philosophers possessed wisdom ["*non defuisse illis sapientiam, si defuit eloquentia*"]. The art of rhetoric requires qualities other than those required by the philosophical speech. "Eloquence is something elegant—that we admit—full of temptations and pleasures, but for a philosopher neither suitable nor welcome."[56]

It appears that Pico is even proud of the bleakness of philosophy, for he says in this connection: "We prefer our unkempt, clumsy and shuffling speech." About the philosopher, he says explicitly that he only cares *what* is written, not *how* it is formulated.[57] These words recall the thesis later expressed by Descartes, that as far as truth is concerned, it is simply a question of evidence, no matter in what language it is expressed.

Thus any doubt about the traditional interpretation of Pico would seem to be untenable. But let us examine his idea of rhetoric a little closer. Quite obviously his criticism of rhetoric refers to a purely "technical," "external" rhetoric, which is able to present any thesis as creditable through the emotive means it uses; that is, his criticism is directed against the kind of rhetoric which Plato objects to with the Sophists. "What is the function of the orator other than to lie, to deceive, to outwit [*quam mentiri, decipere, circumvenire, praestigiare*]? It is truly your work, as you boast, to change black to white and vice-versa at will." Pico also speaks of the well-nigh magic power of rhetoric.[58] In connection with this thesis Pico develops his critique of the "grammarian" insofar as the grammarian idealizes the Roman-Latin language and judges every other language with reference to his standard. As a contrast to this sterile formalism Pico defends Germanic pertinence: "There is probably none who does not prefer the pure gold of Teutonic coinage (meaning rational truth) to false Roman coins (meaning traditional rhetoric)." Once rhetoric becomes a purely "technical" medium to convince, it proves a dangerous weapon in the hands of the ignorant.[59] Seen from this aspect Pico violently objects to it.

Nevertheless Pico is unable to conceal what he *feels* with regard to Barbaro's rhetorical gifts. He even wishes he could express his admiration for Barbaro's fascinating way of speaking and writing: "*Nec possum aut tacere quae de te sentio . . . utinam esset is meae mentis captus, ut pro meritis tuis de te sentirem . . . utinam ea dicendi vis, ut exprimere aliquando possem quod semper sentio.*"[60]

It is strange that the alleged radical opponent of any form of rhetoric should let his feelings run away with him here, and all the more strange that his feeling of admiration is connected particularly to Barbaro's "style." "Your style—to speak of nothing else—for which you care so little, touches me and fills me with a pleasure so wondrous, yes, because it is wise, serious, rounded, erudite, forceful and ingenious."[61] Yet he praises those characteristics of style which point out the content.

We learn, among other things, that Pico and Poliziano are on the search for Barbaro's letters and writings, and that—as it literally says—the reading takes their breath away [*"ut perpetua quadam acclamatione interspirandi locum non habeamus"*]. It is admirable how Barbaro is able to lead the soul whither he wishes through "persuasion."[62] Here it is clear that Pico's previously mentioned criticism of rhetoric is by no means identical with an absolute rejection of any emotive speech, as, for example, later with Descartes.

The Unity of Content and Form in the Originative Philosophical Act

Let us return to Pico's idea of philosophy: *"de humanarum divinarumque rerum rationibus agitur et disputatur."*[63] The philosophy he recognizes starts out with the principles and deals with them. The philosophers that Pico acknowledges do not devote themselves to purely rational knowledge, for they lean on emotive potentialities for effect, by trusting—as Pico expresses himself—not only the tongue but the *heart: "Experietur habuisse barbaros non in lingua sed in pectore Mercurium."* If they would use only formally rhetorical media, then it would mean that they were not sure of their own subject ["*quasi rebus parum fidentes*"].[64] But if the "subject" itself is effective, it does not require an additional, external emotive form. Pico mentions an important example: It is significant that in the holy, sacred writings [*res sacrae*], subject and form are one.

The style in which Pico describes this "archaic" philosophy approaches the language of myths. He talks about the "admiring silence of those few who meditate about something inward, torn either from the grotto of nature or from heaven and transferred to men from the realm of Jupiter."[65]

Thus the theme of the letter shifts. Pico's reference to the Silene of Alcibiades elucidates the nature of genuine philosophy. In outward appearance Silene is coarse and shabby; inwardly, however, she is radiant and precious. Correspondingly he who seeks his schooling with the philosophers must free himself from outward things and turn inward, where God speaks directly: *"Avoca a sensibus, redeas ad te ipsum in animi penetralia mentisque secessus."* Pico continues: "Take the ears of Thianeus, with which, freeing himself from the body, he heard no more worldly Margyas, but only celestial Apollo, who composes on the divine lute with inexpressible harmony the hymns of the universe."[66]

Pico here designs an ideal philosophy, which does not restrict itself to the realm of rational processes; he points to a higher level of philosophizing, in the sense of the Platonic tradition, which the author of *Peri Hupsous* evoked in the age of Hellenism. Following this tradition Pico says of Cicero, in view of his rhetorical accomplishments, that he had demanded from the philosopher a theory whereby the Muse should dwell no longer on the lips, but in the soul [*"habere Musas in animo et non in labris"*].[67]

According to Pico a philosophy or a speech of this kind has an indicative, transforming effect:

> They move not, they convince not [*non movent, non persuadent*], but they *compel*, they *stir*, they *impose* on you a force [*sed cogunt, agitant, vim inferunt*], those words of the Law, rough, simple words, but alive, animated, glowing, sharp [*rudia verba et agrestia, sed viva, sed animata, flammea, aculeata*], penetrating into the depths of the soul, transforming man through a wondrous power.[68]

Pico refers to the statement allegedly stemming from Heraclites, that the philosopher must pursue those words which flow out of the awe-inspiring cave in which the truth lies hidden [*"non ex amoenis Musarum silvis, sed ex horrendo fluxerint antro, in quo dixit Heraclitus latitare veritatem"*]. From this point of view he admits that rhetoric and wisdom are connected with each other, i.e., only on the level of an archaic philosophy in which the impact of the word, that is, the form, represents no external appendix with regard to the content [*"do tibi eloquentiam et sapientiam mutuo nexu invicem conspirasse"*].[69]

Giovanni Pico, in his letter, provides no philosophical foundation for the ideal of an effective philosophy he programmatically designs. The missing foundations are to be found in the works of his nephew, Gianfrancesco Pico. His treatise *De imaginatione* emphasizes the impact of images and contains the theory that, in view of the pictorial nature of the primal, every fundamental speech must be pictorial.

De imaginatione, by Gianfrancesco Pico: Fantastic Images as Guides of Instincts and Passions

As the companion letter of December 1, 1500, states, Gianfrancesco Pico della Mirandola's work *De imaginatione* is dedicated to Emperor Maximilian. It is an attempt to find an answer to the question how the human mind can attain the fundamental union of *res* and *verba*, of "content" and "form." In the framework of this question the author concerns himself particularly with the role of the image, of the mental "appearance," which is designated here with the concepts "fantasy" and "imagination."

Throughout the work the references to Aristotle are obvious. Fantasy, as the gift of imagination, is first generally brought into connection with a "condition of light." ["*Phantasiae nomen de lucis [Gr. phaos = phos] videlicet argumento obtinuit, sine qua videre non est.*"][70] Further, fantasy appears as the soul's power to create images; fantasy itself is fed with the images provided by the senses.[71]

Fantasy, or imagination, assumes an important function. First, it realizes itself in the sphere of the manifold sensory shapes by making a selection of them: "For what meets the senses, that is everything physical as far as it can be distinguished by one of the senses [*quodve ullu sensu sentiri potest*], diffuses a similarity and an image of itself, in imitation of non-physical and spiritual nature [*similitudinem atque imaginem sui quantum potest effundit ad imitationem incorporeae spiritualisque naturae*]."[72] On the other hand the power of the imagination reaches the higher spheres of the mind insofar as it can put at the disposal of the *ratio* and the intellect the images it has acquired through the senses.

The reason why the imagination is so significant for animals as well as men is that it makes instincts and passions possible through the communication of sensory patterns. As Pico says (and here he virtually repeats Aristotelian sentences), "No living being strives toward the unknown."[73] Thus what stirs the passions and guides animal instincts are fantastic images.

Animals, it is true, derive their behavior directly from memory and fantasy because they command no higher faculties. Therefore, according to Gianfrancesco Pico, those shapes that are presented by the imagination have, insofar as they apply to animals and determine organic life, an immediate and unambiguous meaning. Correspondingly, the behavior of animals is always fully adequate and timely.

Preeminence of Imaginative, Indicative Speech over Rational Speech

Man, however, subjects the images of fantasy to his *mens*, his "mind," so that the sensory images are interpreted in a human manner, and accordingly the passions also are interpreted in a human manner. But if man does not submit to the dominion of the *mens*, images and passions become destructive because they are then no longer coordinated in the unequivocal order which discloses the human world.

> For when fantasy has received the images of things from the senses, it contains them in itself, purifies them, and

offers them to the active intellect [*retinet in se, puriores-que effectas offert agenti intellectui*], which illuminates them with its light [*qui suo lumine collustrans*], draws from them the intelligible images [*ab eis intelligibiles species abstrahit*], and deposits them with the latent intellect [*in intellectum potentiae*], which it thus feeds and completes.[74]

Fantasy thereby designs the "potential" meanings of the images, which are then illuminated and defined by the light of the intellect, to be preserved in the mental sphere of man. But the fantastic images might withdraw from this illumination. That is when we experience how, on the one hand, emotionally effective images, and on the other hand, mental contents become autonomous; shape and content, *verba* and *res*, in that case, no longer form a union; the images become misleading and are degraded to mere "appearances." Here lies the root of the arising dualism between content and form.

Thus, according to Gianfrancesco Pico, fantasy must be put under the domain of mental light. That light appears as a divine gift; its function is to reveal the human world.[75] We recall Aristotle's thesis that the first principles, which "clarify" everything, must be recognized as such and believed to a greater extent than what the *ratio*, which is made possible through them, recognizes and believes. For Pico on the basis of this Aristotelian argument, intellectual light and faith form a union. In Chapter 12 of *De imaginatione* he identifies the *lumen nobis congenitum* with the *lumen fidei*, in whose realm language no longer can be rational but only pictorial, i.e., metaphorical. So in this chapter, because it deals with the *archai*, Pico necessarily is forced to speak metaphorically. This is why we find here a new linguistic form which goes beyond the preceding rational argument. The fact that the images of fantasy are "seen" anew in the intellectual light, that the intellectual light itself is not a demonstrable phenomenon, but one demanding "faith," leads Pico to maintain the continuity between fantasy, intellectual light, and faith, and to emphasize that the light of faith is stronger than that of fantasy.[76]

Pico systematically formulates the identity of "intellectual light" and "faith" in his treatise *Examen vanitatis doctrinae gentium*. Here he says: "The heathen philosophers originally gave instructions for faith [*philosophi gentium . . . in principiis itaque praebant praecepta fidei*], of which none of us deny the certainty and some of us admit the evidence [*et sunt qui annuant evidentiam*]."⁷⁷

In *De fide et ordine credenda theoremata* he enumerates the four kinds of light. He begins with the "natural light," from which the original form of faith arises.

> But as the light has been mentioned, it is to be noted that the spiritual light consists of four kinds [*quator haberi spiritualium luminum genera*], which are subordinated to one another. The first is the natural light, as it were the foundation of the other kinds, in which all who possess reason partake [*Primum naturale est veluti basis et fundamentum aliorum, quorum omnes rationis capaces participes sunt*].⁷⁸

As regards our problem we obtain two results. First, if the speech of man depends not only on rational deduction, but above all on the intellectual light, by which the images that appear through the senses are given a human, spiritual meaning, then it is not ultimately rational speech, but noetic, original speech which will gain power over man and achieve the true, moving philosophy.

Second, Pico recognizes precisely the borderline in the human mind where the separation between *res* and *verba* takes place. It is fantasy which effects this separation, if it fails to submit its own fantastic images to the light of noetic insight. In such a case we receive purely "fantastic" images, which still influence the passions, but owing to their severance from "matter," i.e., from the spiritual content, have a predominantly misleading effect. Since animals neither possess nor need any higher faculties, their world is another, the patterns of their fantasy cannot move freely, they have an immediate effect. In the human realm fantasy has the function of leading to cognition, to "seeing." Pico is not interested here in an external, etymological proof, since he connects fantasy by its very nature with the *phos*, "the light." On the other hand the freedom that is specific to it forms the basic element of the human situation; it is only the preservation and transformation of the images supplied by the senses, and of the *pathos* adhering to them, in the scope of the intellectual light, which lead man to his own world. Philosophy in this sense, too, is no longer a rational, deductive process, but an emotive speech guided by insight, which has no rational character and has preeminence.

Conclusion

What is the theoretical background and speculative tradition of such a thesis? My answer to this involves what I have developed in another article.[79]

In the *Posterior Analytics* Aristotle defines knowledge and conviction, i.e., the *rational* belief *[pistis]* arising from demonstration, as follows: "One believes and knows something when a deduction is carried out which we call proof" (*Anal. post.* 72a 25). It is clear that Aristotle here assigns a rational character to the concept of *pistis*, conviction, understanding, and knowledge *[eidenai]* from a special perspective: the determining factor here is *deduction*. Proof consists in "giving the reason." The reason becomes evident in connection with the deduction, which necessarily starts from premises and hence depends on their validity.

Aristotle continues: "Since the conclusion obtains its true validity from the fact that the reason on which it is based is evident, it necessarily follows that with each proof, the first principles in which it has origin must not only be known completely or partially prior to the proof, they *must also be known to a higher degree* than that which is deduced from them" (*Anal. post.* 72a 27).

So when we *know* and *believe* in connection with a proof, we must necessarily *believe* and *know* the premises on which the proof is based *on more forceful grounds*. Aristotle accentuates this fundamental condition: "If we *know and believe* an object by means of the first principle to a more forceful degree than that which is derived from it, *we know and believe* the latter on the basis of the first" (*Anal. post.* 72a 30).

We must be conscious of the change in the meaning of knowledge and belief, as expressed in this passage: here we have a notion of a belief and knowledge, which is more primary than the rational form and of necessity radically different in structure. We must remember, nevertheless, that the nonrational character of the principles are by no means identical with irrationality.

To restate the point made in Chapter 2, in the rational process we claim that we know something when we are able to prove it. To prove *[apo-deiknumi]* means to show something to be something, on the basis of something. It is clear that the first *archai* of any proof and hence of knowledge cannot be proved themselves because they cannot be the object of apodictic, demonstrative, logical speech. The rational process and consequently rational speech must move from the formulation of primary assertions: by using the kind of expression which belongs to the nondeducible they are thoroughly *indicative*. The indicative *[semeinein]* speech provides the framework within which the proof can come into existence. Such speech is immediately a "showing"—and for this reason "figurative" or "imaginative" and thus in the original sense "theoretical" *[theorein*—i.e., to see]. It is metaphorical, i.e., it shows something which has a sense, and this means that to the figure, to that which is shown, the speech transfers *[metapherein]* a signification: in this way the speech which realizes the showing "leads before the eyes" *[phainesthai]* a significance. This speech is and must be in its structure an imaginative language. So according to this humanistic tradition, we are obliged to recognize that every original, former "archaic" speech (archaic in the sense of dominant, *arche, archontes* or the dominants) cannot have a rational but only a rhetorical character. Thus the term "rhetoric" assumes a fundamentally new significance: "rhetoric" is not, nor can it be, the art or the technique of an exterior persuasion: it is rather the speech which is the basis of the rational thought.

This is the reason why Vico, in taking up again the humanistic tradition, affirms that the ground of human historicity and human society is not the rational process of thinking but the imaginative act.

The nature and actuality of Italian Humanism lie in its new conception of philosophical thought. Contrary and in opposition to the logicizing and rationalistic Scholasticism of the late Middle Ages, Humanism examines the nature of man in his concrete, emotive, history-bound evolution, that is, in his historical relevance.

The problem of the origin of society, philosophical reflections in and from history, and the question of the role assumed by fantasy in these matters, are the subjects that occupy the minds of the humanist tradition. The prevalence of practice (to be understood as the starting point of those problems which concern man directly and admit of no postponement) as the recognition that things acquire their meanings in their concrete relationship to man and in man's efforts to cope with them, was possible only by gaining insight into the connections between rhetoric and philosophy, and by rejecting the prevalence of rational language. The new access to a humanist tradition can be brought about neither from a purely *Romanistik* or "history-of-literature" direction, nor by concentrating on points of general history.

Through the problem of the impact of the image, of the difference between rational and allusive language, of the difference between the emotive and the rational word, through the problem of the connection between rhetoric and philosophy, Italian Humanism reaches the crucial question of *what* constitutes historical human reality and *how* this reality can be shaped.

I wish to conclude my inquiry with two quotations—one modern, the other humanistic—which show the actuality of the problem through their parallelism.

> The primary and immediate attitude of man toward reality is not that of an abstract, cognizant subject, a pondering brain with a speculative approach to reality, but that of a perspicuously and practically active being, a historical individual, who performs his practical activity in connection with nature and man, the realization of his motives and interests, in a given complex of social relations. Reality, therefore, does not appear in the human being primarily in the form of an object for contemplation, examination and theorizing, of which the opposite, complementary pole would be the abstract subject of cognizance, but as a sphere of sensuous-practical activity, on the basis of which the direct, practical view of reality develops.[80]

At the end of the humanistic tradition, in a last desperate attempt to reassert its sense and its functions against the traditional conception of metaphysics, and to defend and reinstate it against Descartes's Rationalism, Vico wrote that the philosophers hitherto had considered providence only with regard to natural order, "but they have not yet considered it from the aspect which is peculiar to men, whose nature has that salient characteristic of being sociable." This leads him to the sentence: "But in this night full of shadows covering remotest antiquity from our eyes, there appears the eternal light that does not set, of that truth on which no doubt can be cast—that this historical world has most certainly been made by men and so its principles can be found only in the modifications of our own human spirit."

The new era of philosophy, the Copernican turning point, started neither with Descartes nor with Kant, but with Italian

Humanism. But the consequences resulting from the new evaluation of fantasy, of *ingenium,* of the prevalence of the image, can be discussed only on the basis of a further inquiry into the nature of the Italian humanist tradition. It is the problem of the structure and finality of "topical philosophy."

Rhetoric as the Ground of Society

The Traditional Concept of Scientific Thought

When we look at today's scientific panorama, philosophy hardly appears still to play a role, and rhetorical speech is recognized only outside the framework of scientific discourse as the superficial art of persuasion. The metaphysical claims and aims of philosophy are rejected or relegated to the periphery of scientific concerns. The speculative tradition has petrified, and metaphysics leads a sad existence in the bureaucratically prescribed courses of university curriculums. Logic, structuralism, formal semiotic, and—not the least—sociology add to the critique and rejection of this traditon. It is not our task here to go into this matter. But let it be remembered that it is only within the limits of human communication and the tasks that arise from it that the problems of philosophy and the function of rhetoric can be discussed. Therefore we ask if, on the basis of a new interpretation of rhetoric and its function, philosophy itself can receive an unexpected meaning, and if so, what tradition can be referred to as our starting point?

We must begin with the premise that, whether it be ancient, medieval, or the view that began with Descartes, which we call "modern," all these views of scientific thought begin with the same understanding of science and its method. The differentiation between "traditional" and "modern" thought, in contrast to what we generally believe and maintain, does not mark a change in the basic structure of scientific thought. It is upon this fact that the rejection of rhetoric in science depends. We therefore have the double task of explaining these points and showing that a new model of scientific thought was developed in Italian Humanism, which led to a new evaluation of the function of rhetorical discourse.

In ancient times the basic view was set forth that cognition [episteme, scientia] can be achieved only when our statements [logos] "stand" upon a firm foundation [epistemi]. Thus arose the close conjunction in traditional logic between metaphysics and logic. Only a doctrine of being [*on hei on*], i.e., of what "is" and is generally and necessarily at the basis of everything, can be the origin of our "genuine" statements. Thus arose the necessity of determining the different forms in which man speaks of being [*kategorein*], in order to undertake establishing what appears, the phenomena, in a manner that is well founded. Seen from this point of view the fundamental problem of logic is, for one thing, conjunction, i.e., the structure of the unity of the subject and what is said about it or predicated of it. This is the problem that Aristotle examined in the *Prior Analytics* as the rational process of derivation. Logic must explain the nature of reasons, the original premises from which each derivation begins; and this is the problem that Aristotle examined in the *Second Analytics*.

For these reasons the three essential elements of a rational proposition are important for such a logic: the concept [*horos*], the definition [*horismos*], and the rational process of inference. The *concept* must hold or grasp the maniford nature of the phenomena in a unity. The *definition* refers this multiplicity back to the original unity, i.e., the genus in which it "rests," and then expresses the specific difference which it exhibits within the genus. In this way the phenomenon that is to be defined is anchored in its general and necessary meaning and expressed in its conceptual essence. The definition expresses this "fixed" and "founded" generality. "The Definition [*horismos*] is the assertion [*logos*] which is rooted in distinctions."[1] Let us not forget in this regard that the meaning of *horos*, i.e., to limit, has an identical root *hor* with the verb *horao*, to see or look. In other words here we have to do with seeing the phenomena in regard to the way they are anchored in a general "ground" and in a meaning that is thus exclusively "universal." Everything individual and bound to space and time, therefore, *cannot* be grasped in this way. Accordingly because it begins with situations bound up in space and time, *rhetorical speech cannot be scientific language.*

Let us consider the reasons, according to the previously mentioned interpretation, that led to the rejection of rhetorical speech in the Middle Ages as a scientific mode of expression. John Scotus (810-877) says he offers no presentation of grammar and rhetoric "because they do not appear to have to do with the nature of things, but rather either with the laws of the human voice, which according to the view of Aristotle and his followers deal not with nature but with the habits of speech, or particular objects and persons, *which is far removed from the nature of things.*"2

The "nature of things" mentioned here is rooted on this view in necessary and general "reasons" that also represent their original causes. The constantly changing phenomena remain illusions until they are traced back in their definitions to their reasons. Essential reality, the "nature of things," stands above (or behind) the manifold, particular, different, and relative as the general or universal that must be *purified* through cognition from all of these qualities. "The variety of customs and social forms also comes from the environment, from times and places, procreation, the nature and amount of food, locale, and atmosphere . . . in brief, from all that comes to some stability without itself being what is stabile."3

For medieval rationalistic thought insight and language thus are anchored in universally valid reasons and derivable only from them. For Abelard (1079-1142) thought, speech, and action only represent a "reconstruction" of the human world with regard to what always exists without change. It aims at the composition [*componere*] of existence according to eternal principles and causes or to infer it from these and to formulate it accordingly in a language that is scientific insofar as it has this *rational character*. Language should reflect the hierarchical order of being, not individual situations such as the state of the passions in respect to something that occurs "here" and "now."

> We do not call every science philosophy nor every knowledgeable person a philosopher, but rather only those who stand out in the precision of their insight [*subtilitate intelligentiae praeeminentes*] and who make careful distinctions in regard to that which they know [*diligentem habent discretionem*]. The capacity to make distinctions is a possession of those who can grasp and evaluate the hidden causes of things. We call causes hidden when the things that come from them are to be considered more through the understanding than experience through the senses. Alone the senses are equally distributed to the stupid, to men capable of making distinctions, and to animals.4

Contemporary logic's interest in medieval logic is understandable because medieval logic also stresses the point that scientific discourse and thought can be sought and found only within the framework of proofs. But modern logic does not go as far, since it indicates that the premises of a formal logical proof cannot be proven and so logic can have only a *formal* character. If we rely on "intuition" or the "evidence" of the premises, we surrender ourselves to arbitrariness and subjectivism and, in contrast to the speculative medieval view, find no way to go from logic to metaphysics and hence to philosophy.

Modern thought begins with Descartes, who founded philosophy and thereby scientific thought on the *cogito* instead of on a doctrine of being, but he does *not abandon* the model of scientific thought that we have been discussing. For Descartes it is the model of mathematical thought, the "evidence" of principles and axioms and the propositions that can be deduced from them that guarantee scientific objectivity. Problems are solved through proofs that reflect the mathematical and geometric premises upon which they are based, "the long chain of simple and plain reasons like the geometer is used to using. . . ."[5] The starting point for philosophy—the *cogito*— is new, compared to the Middle Ages, but in no way does it redefine the structure of scientific thought.

This is true for Kant as well. Kant stressed that empirical experience, which begins with the object, teaches that something is constituted in one way or another but not that it can be no other way. Thus Kant's "critical" turn; science can be completed if it is possible to find a priori forms of knowledge in ourselves and to infer knowledge from them. The experience of reality is derived on different levels from forms of human consciousness that are transcendental matters of fact. In this way Kant's so-called Copernican revolution rests upon the basic traditional concept of scientific thought.

The mathematical model is retained in the idealistic tradition. Fichte holds that all coherent propositions must be rooted in *one basic proposition* from which all the derivable consequences are drawn. Hegel was convinced that through Descartes the philosophy of the modern world came about because it "knows that it comes from reason without outside help and that self-consciousness is an essential aspect of the truth." And so Hegel rejects every attempt that does not meet the demands of the Idea, and he claims that the attempt to come back to the world of fantasy or art within scientific thought is irrelevant. Because of this, rhetoric has no place in philosophy. "The clumsiness of trying to represent thought as thought grabs for help from the expedient of expressing itself in sensory form."[6]

Works and Words as the Sources of Human History

The humanist tradition denies the primacy of logic and its language. It takes rhetoric as the starting point for philosophizing and attains a new understanding of scientific thought which no longer is identified with derivations from necessary and universal premises. It breaks with the mathematical ideal of knowledge.

In order to understand this tradition we are forced to refer to various authors and considerations that at first glance hardly seem to have a relationship to the questions we have been discussing, since they deal with the problem of the origin of the human community and the political function of poetry. As far as poetry is concerned we must note that it makes use of metaphors and images that affect the passions and lend it a rhetorical function.

Our historical discussion begins before Humanism, at the end of the Middle Ages, when the beginnings of a new way of thought can be discerned. It is understandable that, on the basis of the model of cognition we have been discussing, which is still predominant today, these authors are recognized as important primarily from the point of view of literary history but are considered of no real importance for speculative thought. I want to consider most of all Brunetto Latini, Dante's teacher, and then Dante's views of the function of poetry as an aspect of rhetorical speech, the poet as orator.

In his *Tresor,* which is the first medieval *summa* that was written in the people's tongue (Provençal) instead of Latin, Brunetto Latini (1220–1294) presents the fundamental thesis that politics has primacy under all forms of knowledge *[artes]*. He does not consider thereby the notion of politics to be restricted to the art of government but rather understands it as every activity that has to do with unfolding man's nature and the rise of the community.

According to Latini's view two forms of human activity lie at the basis of politics: *work*—he specifies a number of occupations in this treatise with which man transforms nature in order to satisfy his needs—and the *word.*

> Politics . . . is the highest science and the loftiest activity of men. It is that which teaches us how to rule a people, a state, or a group in times of war and peace. It teaches us all the arts and occupations *[mestiers]* that man needs *[ki a vie d'ome sont besonable]*. And it achieves this in two

ways; one is through work [*oeuvre*], the other is through words [*paroles*]. What it achieves through work occurs through the occupations of blacksmith, weaver, farm worker . . . all occupations that man needs. . . . What man achieves through *words* occurs through his mouth and his tongue.[7]

For Latini "word" means language, both in its prosaic looseness and in poetic form where expressions are ordered through rhythm and melody, i.e., lower and higher tone levels. He associates both forms of language with rhetoric whereby he of course stresses "that speech in prose is large and full like the way most people speak. The path of rhyme, however, is narrow and powerful [*clos et fermés*] like something that is contained by walls and palisades, that is, by weight, measure, and unequivocal number [*de pois et de nombre et de mesure*], which man neither can nor may overstep." Latini adds a further essential characteristic of poetic language to this list by writing: "The order of artistic speech does not keep to the trodden path but takes narrow gangways and approaches that lead him [the poet] directly to the goal that he wants to reach. He does not say the way each thing was; he even changes what came first, in the middle, or afterwards—not by chance, but on purpose in order to make his intention clear."[8]

Latini mentions explicitly Cicero's view that the poet has a unique and original capacity, i.e., he creates the human community and human history. Latini writes:

> Tuilles dit que au commencement qu li home vivoient a loi de bestes, sans propres maisons et sans cognoissance de Dieu, parmi le bois et parmi le repostailles champetres, si ke nus n'i regar doit mariage nus ne connissist peres ne fiz. Lors fu uns sages hom bien parlans, ki tant consilla le autres et tant lor moustra la grandour de l'ame et la dignité de la raison et de la discretion, qu'il les restraist de ce sauvegines, et les aombra a abiter en i. lieu et a garder raison et justice. Et ensi por la bonne parleur ki en lui estoit acompaignie o sens fu cesti ausi comme i. secons Dieus, ki estora le monde par l'ordene de l'humaine compaignie.[9]

Latini's comments probably are related to the following passage from Cicero's *De inventione:*

For there was a time in which men roamed over the fields

like wild animals [*in agris homines passim bestiarum modo vagabantur*], lived from the food that grew wild, and acted according to the powers of the body rather than the mind [*nec ratione animi quidquam, sed pleraque viribus corporis administrabant*]. They had neither divine religion nor human duties. No one paid attention to lawful marriages; no one viewed children with certainty as their own [*nemo nuptias viderat legitimas; non certos quisquam inpexerat liberos*]. . . . In this way, through ignorance and error, the passions of the soul—a blind and aimless ruler—misused the powers of the body—a dangerous servant.[10]

Human society originates in the poet as orator and in work. We have reproduced the passages from Latini and Cicero because they are nearly verbatim what Giambattista Vico will say in his *New Science* hundreds of years later when he speaks about the origin of human society.[11]

The problem facing us is to determine the importance of Latini's views and, if they have a philosophical meaning, what follows from this as far as the function of rhetoric is concerned. Several historical references are necessary here in order to understand the source of the tradition that sees the origin of human society in poetry and metaphoric thought. In his oration *Pro archia*, Cicero proposes that art and poetry may not be taken as expressions of individual talent because they are rooted in the field of objectivity and in the sacred.[12] In this way the true meaning and function of the "remembering" is found that typifies the poet because of his relationship to what is original. The memory which is typically a possession of poets allows that which is glorious and famous to reappear through the poet and relates later generations to these "examples." That is, the poet thereby fulfills a basic, essential, historical, and political task.

By means of the extolling statements made by the poets, the memory is activated in the soul because the historical facts that it represents are shown to be "examples." Cicero says: "Thus in a city (like Rome) where the generals still honored the temple of the muses and almost carried the name 'poet' in the decorations of their weapons [*imperatores prope armati poetarum nomen et Musarum delubra coluerunt*], even the judges dressed in the garments of peace could not escape honoring and preserving the poets [*non debent togati iudices a Musarum honore et poetarum salute abhorrere*]."[13]

The second political task of poetry is seen in the fact that art, including poetry, through its means—tones, words, images—affects the passions and reveals a relationship to the kind of rhetoric that leads to actions and the realization of political ends. This is precisely the thesis that Horace proposes in his "Letter to the Pisons" about the close relationship between art, rhetoric, and the development of the human community with its order and institutions. For Horace poetry is that primary force that is able to overcome the chaos in which men originally live. It is the means by which the order of a human society develops. The poets are named *vates,* "revealers" or seers, because they see new possible human relationships in an original underived manner and give birth to these possibilities. Horace, like Latini, refers to the role of the poet in the ancient tradition and to the fabulous achievements of Orpheus and Amphion. Orpheus attracted men from the wilderness with music and brought them by means of his art to form a human community. Amphion brought stones into movement through his music for the construction of Thebes and arranged them with regard to the end of making a civil society. His goal was political in nature because the city walls are the border with external chaos, nature which man has not yet made to serve himself, which he has not yet "humanized."[14]

Musike—not music, but the organizing power of the muses and poets—creates the measure for everything that is not merely "outside" of man in the form of "external nature," but which also manifests itself in him, in his drives and passions. Poetic, figurative, and hence "metaphorical" activities provide the possibility of mankind liberating itself from the immediate strictures of nature. This possibility proves itself in the "festival"; humanity is celebrated in the freedom that is attained in the power of the metaphor.[15]

With this, "knowledge" is attributed to the poet as orator. The measure or criterion which he provides serves to realize the essence of man by developing and ordering the passions in the family and by regulating the relationships between men in the order of the state.[16] In this regard the function of art and poetry is its "usefulness" [*prodesse*] in the construction of the human world. But what elements explain the role of rhetoric here when Latini refers to work and the word as the sources of human history and extends the tradition of the poet as orator to include poetic action?

Poeta as Orator

The problem confronting us is that our rationalistic scientific ideal of knowledge equates the rigor of objective thought with the provable and excludes every form of figurative, poetic, metaphorical, and rhetorical language from the theoretical sphere. From this fact three questions arise: (1) whether such an exclusion is legitimate; (2) what is the importance of a tradition like the humanistic one, whether we accept or reject it, that is based upon the assertion of the primacy of figurative language as the source of the historicity characteristic of human beings; and (3) the problem of whether the questions and theories of the humanist tradition permit overcoming the purely logical and "formalistic" character of contemporary thought.

To continue to approach these problems historically, I want to refer to Dante's two writings, *De vulgari eloquentia* and *Convivio,* where the notion of the poet as orator is shown in all of its implications. Dante defines poetic language as "a rhetorical idea presented in music" *[fictio rhetorica musicaque poita].* For Dante *fictio* means "idea" and *fingere* is identical with *imaginare.*[17] The participle *poita* comes from the archaic verb *poire* and is related etymologically to the Greek work *poiesis. Poiesis* has as its basic meaning the production of something that alters nature and does not contain its goal in itself. It is a work that is made for either its usefulness or enjoyment. *Fiction rhetorica* means an invention that acts expressively, as does the art of speech. It aims at the unity, interconnection, and order of the parts, and finally at reproduction of and influence on the passions. The connection with music that Dante mentioned refers to the rhythm of the verse and the structured, bound character of poetic language.[18]

According to Dante's definition language arises as a question or an answer *[vel per modum interrogationis, vel per modum responsionis]* in the context of some material or spiritual imposition of need. The imposition manifests itself as a task, and it is only in reference to this task that reality, as it is open to our sense organs, receives its meaning. Two aspects of this are important here; on the one hand the conveyance of meanings to sensory appearances, i.e., the activity of *meta-pherein,* and on the other hand the imposition of a tension and "attention" *[tendere ad].* According to Dante the original, i.e., the divine, manifests itself in this original tension.[19] Here the whole importance of Dante's theory of language will become apparent, which is why it now must be discussed fully.

The decisive step in Dante's reflections occurs with the assertion that originally, in an unhistorical time before man's revolt against God—symbolized for Dante in the construction of the tower of Babel—there was only a single language for all men. The fragmentation of this original language begins with the erection of the tower of Babel and, what is essential to this, work—the variety of differently structured activities. For Dante work means to convey a meaning to natural things and thereby to transform them with regard to some particular yet unattained goal. In the concrete case which concerns us here the erection of the tower is meant. In other words every job that arises from the necessity of fulfilling a particular task defines reality and becomes the source of "naming."

The origin of work, from which the different languages develop, is effort. This is articulated according to the yet unattained aim of "humanizing" nature. According to Dante's view this "humanization" begins with the revolt against the originally existing order which thereby is lost and then built up anew in a different way. Here is the origin of human historicity.

Dante writes that with the construction of the tower of Babel part of the people

> commanded, a part were master builders, a part put up walls, a part dressed them with edging . . . so that although they originally used one and the same language, this became divided into many languages in the course of this work and when the people left this project they never returned to the same mutual understanding. Only those who were united by the same activity were left with the same language [*solis etenim in uno convenientibus actu eadem loquela remansit*]. There was one for master builders, another for all the stonerollers. . . . For all the different tasks that were present at that project there arose different languages which led to the disintegration of the unity of the human race [*tot idiomatibus tunc genus humanum disiungitur*].[20]

In this new situation of revolts wherein history comes into being, Dante discerns two kinds of language. The first kind is ahistorical and artificial, a language in which the different languages of the different peoples has been crystallized, so to speak, according to fixed rules. This, for Dante, is the universal language—Latin. He also calls this language "grammatical" because on his view it is constructed in a purely rational way and so is ahistorical.

> The inventors of the art of Latin [*grammaticae facultatis*] began here. The aforementioned Latin is nothing other than the unchang[e]able unity of language at different times and places [*inalterabilis locutionis identitas diversis temporibus atque locis*]. Since this is regulated through the joint agreement of many peoples, it is not yet subject to the will of an individual and so is unchanging [*nulli singulari arbitrio videtur obnoxia, et per consequens nec variabilis esse potest*]. It was invented so that we can avoid losing access to the authority and acts of the far removed ancients and their followers through the differences of language which result when the will of the individual can change it in one way or another [*ne propter variationem sermonis arbitrio singularium fluitantis*].[21]

The great Latin poets conceived their works in this language which is safe from historical changes.

The important task which Dante took upon himself stems from this consciousness of his mission as a poet. He claims that "true," "authentic" language can never be "artificial" or "fixed" (he is referring to Latin) but only one in which men work, act, and live—that language in which they express their strivings and passions that stem from a concrete situation. He means the second kind of language, the particular people's native tongue in all its historicity. "The people's tongue is all the closer to us the more we are associated with it. For it is this alone that is then close to us, and not in any accidental way, but because it is connected with the people that are closest to us, our relatives, fellow-citizens, and our own people. This is our native tongue which is not just close to us personally, but near to everyone of us."[22]

The "authenticity" of the language that the poet as *vates* or "orator" realizes can be found and identified only in the multiplicity of different dialects that are the expression of a particular historical situation. Dante describes the first phase of this task, which never before has been formulated in such a programmatic and conscious way by a poet, as a hunt for a panther that is hidden in a thicket in the forest, in the bush of different dialects. This metaphor expresses Dante's view that a multiplicity of formulations results in different rhythms, standards, and orders that are all needed in order to make possible the community that is necessary for life in different situations. "After we hunt through Italy's forests and fields and have not found the panther we seek, we want to look for it according to a plan so that we can trap in our net this creature whose scent is everywhere but is seen nowhere [*redolentem ubique et nec ubi apparentem*]."[23]

Dante also tells about the dangers of this hunt, which consist in the fact that it cannot be guided properly and objectively whenever the person who is engaged in it is seduced by an inclination to his own dialect. The following quotation reveals the danger of this lack of objectivity in all of its drama. Dante writes:

> We, however, whose home is the world like the fish's is the sea [*Nos autem, cui mundus est patria velut piscibus equor*], although we drank from the Arno before we had teeth and loved Florence so much that we can withstand our banishment because of this love, prefer to strengthen the back of our judgement through reason rather than through feeling. Although there is no more imposing place on earth for the pleasure or contentment of our senses than Florence [*quamvis ad voluptatem nostram sive nostre sesualitatis quietem in terris amoenior locus quam Florentia non existat*], we went through the volumes of the poets and other writers in which the world is described generally and in detail. We evaluated the many kinds of places in the world and their relationship to both poles and the equator. And so we came to the conclusion that there are a number of places and cities that are more noble and picturesque than Tuscany and Florence from whence I come and where I am a citizen and that many nations and people possess a happier and more useful language than the Italians.[24]

Dante believes that the sought-after objective and true language can be found only where man's self-realization is expressed in his confrontation with nature, that is, in work, in communication with others, and in the face of his own passions, in short, in language as the expression of historicity.

Beginning with this insight Dante develops his great thesis that as a poet, i.e., as the one who creates the meaning of reality through his own assignment of this meaning, he will complete this task. However, this task can be completed only when the poets assign meanings with regard to the formation of society and its future. The language needed for this task must use images and metaphors because this is the only way that it can affect the passions. The poet must be an orator. It is doubtful that a poet has ever made the claim to be able *by virtue of his own powers* to produce a "true" language in the jungle of feelings, different actions, and aims by which it then would be possible to "humanize" nature without and within us through the assignment of meanings. Dante's attitude toward this task is clear when he writes:

> And I give this honor to this friend [i.e., the people's language] by openly revealing that which is present in it as something hidden and possible, namely in its true achievement, the manifestation of conscious statements [*E questa grandezza dò io a questo amico, in quanto elli di bontade avea in podere ed occulto, lo fo avere in atto e palese nella sua propria operazione, che è manifestare conceputa sentenza*].[25]

Those who do not recognize this task and who utilize "foreign," untrue language are anathema for Dante. "To the eternal disgrace and degradation of the evil people of Italy who recommend other people's native tongue and are contemptuous of their own, I say that their behavior comes from five disgusting causes."[26]

The "genuine" original language out of which human society develops is therefore imagistic and directive, not argumentative. It is the language created by the poet as orator and *vates* who defines a historical area with his speech. Picturesque language is essentially metaphorical insofar as it "humanizes" the real through the assignment of meanings in the framework of the tasks whereby man realizes himself in different periods of time. Here is the primacy of directive, revelatory, metaphorical language over argumentative, deductive, rational speech.

For Dante four characteristics of the sought-after "rhetorical language" result from answering such questions as arise in certain situations with regard to the future and its relationship to certain needs and aims. Most of all we see here the political function that such a language must possess. At the same time the rhetorical basis is unmistakable in the work of the poet who assumes this task. Dante remarks with bitterness that it is only out of love for this oratorical and political task that he has to wander about Italy like a refugee.

> I passed as a wanderer through all those parts where this language is found [*peregrino, quasi mendicando sono andato*], nearly begging, and against my will I have

shown the wounds of my fate which are very unjustly blamed on the one who is wounded. In fact I was a ship without sails and without a rudder, led to different ports, river outlets, and beaches by every dry wind that accompanies the pains of poverty [*veramente io sono stato legno senza vela e senza governo, portato a diversi porti e foci e liti dal vento secco che vapora la dolorosa povertà*]. And I appeared before many who certainly had had another image of me because of a measure of fame that had [preceded] me. In their eyes not only my person grew smaller, but my work as well, including what I had accomplished and have yet still to complete.[27]

Dante enumerates four features that a "genuine" language must have. They indicate how poetic metaphorical language must be understood in its historical political function. *Illustre* is the first characteristic of the language that Dante seeks and wants to realize in his own work because of the political and historical situation in which he lives. *Illustre* could be translated as "famous" or "exalted," but I believe that these adjectives do not express the quality that Dante has in mind. This requires that the verb be rendered *illustrare,* as "illuminating" in the sense that language brings men to an insight into higher truths and the movements of the soul by virtue of the "illuminating brilliance" of its creative poetic power. In other words genuine language must stem from the depths of human creativity, be directed to all aspects of humanity, and lead to spiritual and practical self-realization. Only this way can it also embrace and advance men's political life as well. This interpretation is corroborated by a passage in *De vulgari eloquentia* where *illustre* is explained. Dante writes: "*Per hoc quoque quod illustre dicimus, intelligimus quid illuminare et illuminatum praefulgens.*"[28]

The second feature that Dante attributes to the sought-after language he names with the adjective *cardinale.* The English translation "authoritative" is pale and weakens the power of the image that is contained in this word. For just as a door receives firm support from its hinge [*cardo*] and thereby is able to move with ease, so the multitude of different dialects can resonate together only in relationship to the ideal model that the poet establishes. How else can the positive features of the many different dialects be judged and brought to life? "Doesn't it [the poetic capacity] exterminate the thorny bushes day by day from the Italian forest? Doesn't it daily sow plants and lay out a garden? What else do its laborers do but clean out and renew in this way?"[29]

By means of the third feature, which Dante designates as *aulica*, the people's tongue finds its way into the royal court. The court [*aula*] presents the "ideal" place for the art of the poet to be judged and given its due. We must remember, however, that the historical and political situation in which Dante lived was distinguished by the *absence* of a real political center or "court" where such an ideal language could have been accepted and encouraged. "Hence it is that our illustrious language wanders about like a foreigner and only finds lodging in the lesser cities since we possess no royal court."[30]

Dante recognized the historical situation in which he lived. If Italy had a royal court, a political center, then the poet would have a place appropriate to his poetic oratorical task. But because there was no such place, it became a purely ideal notion, an ideal *aula* in which the different poet-orators sought a footing. Despite this insight into the historical situation Dante retained the hope that the political goal and ideal of a monarchy one day would become reality. The man who embodied this hope for him was Henry VII, the possible emperor and king of Italy. One of Dante's letters says, "So wake up, all of you and go to your king, men of Italy, not just for the Empire, but as a free people, who are destined to rule."[31]

The last feature of the sought-after language Dante calls the *curiale* of language. *Curia* is the place where the law is established and holds sway. *Curialitas* is itself the quality of balance and measure in rules of action [*curialitas nil aliud est quam librata regula eorumque peragenda sunt*].[32] In Dante's terminology *curiale* language stems from those normative actions and institutionalizations that form the foundations of the human community, i.e., from judgments and norms that provide the basis for balanced law, which when pursued, protects everyone's interests and welfare.

> Even though we have no royal house in Italy in the sense that it alone is recognized like the royal house of the German kings, the needed members are not lacking. And just [as] the members of the German royal house are united by a single prince, so the members of our royal house are united by the light of reason. So it would be false to say that Italians have no royal house, even though we have no prince.[33]

The Humanistic Problems

The poet as orator calls the human world into being and realizes it for the sake of the word, through the word as rhetorical. But the objection remains that the world that comes into being through the poet cannot be the object of science because it is based on metaphors. Scientific thought precludes accepting such a presupposition, since it represents something that is "merely human." Metaphors represent a merely picturesque beginning for thought in unfounded and unfoundable guideposts within a darkness that is impenetrable for men. This objection leads to the rejection of the humanist tradition as "empty." Does it not offer us a "subjective" world if it is based upon principles [*archai*] that cannot be proved rationally? Metaphors reduce themselves to a mysterious "game" that scientific thought never can grasp.

Here certain historical references are again necessary. The interpretation of metaphors as original forms of giving meaning or indicators goes back to ancient times and stretches into the present. Even Homer's work was interpreted as a kind of book of wisdom in code. Metrodorus of Lambsacos (fifth century B.C.) equates the Homeric gods with the four basic elements of the world, with air, earth, fire, and water. The meaning of this allegory is amplified by the Stoics. According to Zeno (336-264 B.C.) the Titans stand for the elements of the cosmos. And in the first century before Christ Cornutus—for example—assumes that Homer and Hesiod hand down an "older" secret wisdom in a figurative, imagistic form. The Neoplatonists (Philo, Porphyry, Proclus) continually make use of allegories.[34]

Since its beginnings Christianity has built up a system of allegory for the interpretation of the Old and New Testaments. In the Middle Ages Isidore of Seville (died 635) wrote in his *Etymologiarum sive originum libri* that the poet is to be viewed as a *vates* or "seer" because of the underived nature of his poetic capacities.[35] Poetic metaphors connect sensory appearances in order to assign to them unexpected meanings which would be unattainable for rational thought.

Fulgentius (sixth century) writes in his commentary *De continentia vergiliana* that Vergil himself appeared to him in order to explain that he had created a metaphor of human life in the twelve books of the *Aeneid*.[36] Bernardus Silvestris puts forth the thesis that Vergil's work contains a twofold wisdom [*gemina doctrina*], a philosophical one that proceeds from his doctrines,

and a poetic one that is seen in his fictions [*figmenta*].[37] Vergil
liberates himself through these fictions, as Silvestris comments,
from the material of historical dates in order to attain a higher
truth "disguised" in images. Under the cover [*integumentum*] of
"fable" he shows the creations of the human mind. This cover,
the image, is utilized as a type of demonstration [*integumentum
verum est genus demonstrativum*]. The "true" is shown in a fable
in its immediate underived meaning [*sub fabulae narratione
veritatis involvens intellectum*]. The value of these works consists in the fact that images help people to attain self-knowledge.[38]
When we ignore the complex of questions that comes to the fore
in connection with this definition of poetic works and their
function, attempts at allegorical interpretation seem to be pure
madness, as Comparetti showed in his well-known investigation
of *Vergil in the Middle Ages*.[39]

In order to answer the question whether or not metaphor
reduces to a "game" without scientific value, and to keep the
humanistic position on this problem before us, I want to turn to
De laboris Herculis by Coluccio Salutati (1331-1406), Petrarch's
student and the first political chancellor of Florence. In this
work the author defends the political role of metaphorical
speech and hence poetry itself. Boccaccio (1313-1375) had already emphasized the rhetorical emotional character and historical political function of poetry in his *Genealogia deorum*.
Poetry "transfigures" the primitivism of people in that it lends
to their behavior a measure which is the basis of human society.
Boccaccio adds that the ties which poetry brings with it are
related to the original binding [*re-ligio*] of people in a society.

Salutati's work about the "labor of Hercules" does not
show at first glance what the person of Hercules can have to do
with an investigation of the essence of poetry and its function.
In order to understand why Salutati refers to Hercules to defend
poetry, we must remember that the ancient tradition saw him as
the *heros* who founded cultural and ethical values. This is why
his picture was used to decorate schools. He was seen and
honored as the victor who controlled the forces of nature, the
protector of inventions like navigation, the designer of high-
ways, and the founder of cities. According to Plutarch, Hercules learned the alphabet from Protheus in Egypt and taught it
to the Greeks. Vergil's commentator in the sixth century,
Servius, declares him to be the founder of the sciences.

Hercules' works, through which he attained immortality,

let him stand as an example for people. The Sophist Prodicus tells the parable of Hercules at the Bivium. The young hero stands before two paths, the path of lust, which is effortless, and the path of capabilities, which is laborious. He chooses the path of capabilities by which he attains immortality.

Like Prodicus, Antisthenes interprets the struggle of Hercules with wild animals as the victory of reason over the passions; this is the reason that the Stoics honored him. This tradition extends into Christianity where Justinus interprets Hercules as Christ's predecessor and Dio Chrisostomus refers to him as the model of human effort and freedom.[40] Hercules helps, punishes, and educates.

When Salutati plans the defense of poetry and hence of metaphorical expression by going back to Hercules, it is obvious that he does not view poetry as a "game" but as an essential aspect of human self-realization. He begins his discussion by maintaining that poetry is politically and thus historically important. He criticizes Plato, who excludes the poets from the state that he, the philosopher, "thought up" and that has never existed [*"istos (poetas) ex illa solum urbe depulit cuius statum nullo modo videre potuit sed confinxit"*].[41]

He refers to Thyrtaios, Euripedes, and Sophocles in order to prove that there was always a close relationship between poetry and the art of government. This reference to Thyrtaios and other poets gives proof of Salutati's thesis that *"non solum non pulsi de civitate fuerint sed inter principes administrande rei publice sint recepti, prepositi bellis, et regum asciti consiliis, ut iuxta determinationes ipsorum maximorum regnorum negocia gererentur."* As an example he mentions the relationship between Euripides and Archeliseus, king of Macedonia, who left the development and decision-making process on all projects to Euripides.[42]

All of these references are only an introduction to Salutati's fundamental thesis about the political role of poetry. He introduces this by noting that poetry is attained only by peoples who have reached a great religious feeling and rhetorical capacity [*"Nam huius artis initium a viris eloquentissimis atque secundum sua tempora et nationem religiosissimis sine dubio creditur provenisse"*].[43]

Poetry helps mankind to overcome the *ferinitas* by lifting the examples of such creators to heaven [*"(Poetae) volentes popularem multitudinem in eorum quos laudabant ad-*

mirationem inducere non plano orationis genere sed verba pro verbis et res pro rebus suavissime commutantes audientes populos a sensibus taliter traducebant"].[44]

In this way poetry has the power to lead human beings beyond the senses so that a discrepancy arises between what the senses perceive and this new revealed truth [*contrarium visibiliter percepissent*]. Salutati proves the fruitfulness of poetry by pointing to this "new" reality. The reality of human society is the highest good, in Salutati's opinion, whether it be compared to either private or public life. This fact forces us to accept the high place of poetry. [*"Nam etsi nichil tante utilitatis vel privatim vel publice cogitari queat quo talis error foret mortalibus persuadendus et aliqua sacrilege superstitionis impietas cogitanda, satis tamen debet humana fragilitas rudibus illis viris quibus se nondum divinitas revelaverat indulgere."*][45]

The fundamental function of assigning metaphorical meanings is thus the work of Hercules for the development of the human world. The meaning of poetry is derived here not through argument but by reference to a fact. Language fulfills the function that Giambattista Vico several centuries later attributes to it. The first language is full of fantasy, imagistic, directive in nature, and not rational or argumentative.

The humanist tradition excludes every kind of "formalism" from "genuine" language. The essential elements leading to the human world are work and fantasy. Work is the continuing attempt to meet human needs through the means provided by the *artes*. Experience teaches us that the various needs and questions that stem from human freedom (insofar as man, in contrast to animals, is not bound to innate schemata through which nature is interpreted) form the *archai* or presuppositions of every interpretive activity on the basis of which work becomes possible. The pressing nature and meaning of every question and answer, its concrete character, which is the root of the human world, is excluded from every formalistic approach to language. But it is only in this concrete context that truth and error, inquiry and knowledge receive their meaning.

If we should draw one preliminary conclusion from what has been said so far, this point would have to be stressed. In the tradition that we have been discussing, figurative language, metaphor, and so every immediate, imagistic, and rhetorical form of speech is of fundamental importance. The fact that this primary importance of rhetorical speech has been misunderstood and concealed is one of the reasons for the devaluation of Italian Humanism.

We must therefore show the importance of the metaphor in the framework of Humanism itself. With Cristoforo Landino (1424–1498) the use of the metaphor is elevated to a method of knowing. In his inaugural lecture at the *Studio fiorentino* in 1458, when he assumed the chair for rhetoric and poetry, Landino asserted that poetry and metaphor had a priority over all the *artes*. He claimed that poetry encompasses all of the free or "liberal" arts, i.e., the Trivium and the Quadrivium. "I am not going to maintain that poetry is one of the arts that the ancients called 'free,' but that one that encompasses all of the others. It translates in an invisible way the things that have already been made into a well measured verse and beautifies them in a number of ways."[46]

In order to understand the implications of these comments, we must remember the medieval division of the sciences into the Trivium and Quadrivium of the seven "liberal arts." The Quadrivium contains arithmetic, geometry, astronomy, and music. Its four paths [*methodos:* method] lead to theory insofar as its arts reflect a fixed, constant order in *number and measure*. Music belongs to these because, in accordance with the medieval point of view, music does not express subjective, relative moods and feelings but rather reveals the lawful nature of the world in rhythm and tone. The Trivium of grammar, logic, and rhetoric has to do with the *word*, communication. By referring poetry to rhetoric, i.e., the art of making human historicity through the word, the task of the poet and orator becomes identical; the poet's task is political.

Now, since on the medieval view the Trivium—the way of the *word*—and the Quadrivium—the way of the *number*—encompass all knowledge, Landino's thesis is that poetry with its imagistic metaphorical character has primacy over all forms of knowledge. Here the question arises of how we are to understand Landino's thesis, since he comes to this theoretical issue in his commentary on Vergil's *Aeneid*, i.e., through the interpretation of a poetic work, in the midst of the *Camaldolenian Discussions* where his problem is the relationship between theory and practice. Does this mean that the poet reaches an insight that the philosopher as the representative of rational thought never achieves?

Landino's view is stated plainly and clearly in the first pages of the lecture where he presents his argument. His task is to prove "what poetry is, whence it originates, but also the way it has always everywhere been honored, and finally, what value it has and how it has not merely been an ornament for particular individuals but whole states and peoples."[47]

Landino discusses Plato's theory of "divine madness" in order to explain the "transformation to a new genus" that is a characteristic of poetry. He quotes the *Tusculanae* as well: "*Mihi vero ne haec quidem notiora et inlustriora carere vi divina videntur, ut ego aut poetam grave plenumque carmen sine caelesti aliquo mentis instinctu putem fundere.*" The doctrine of divine madness that is at the basis of poetry goes back to the notion that knowledge lies in the "recollection" of that which the soul originally saw when it subsisted in the original underived state, that sphere "in which we see the ideas and the images of what God created, as in a mirror."[48]

When we recall that Landino asserted the primacy of poetry over the "liberal arts"—those arts that present the different paths to knowledge—then the "madness" in which poetry is rooted assumes the function of "fantastic induction." That is, here induction is not the result of abstraction from a multiplicity, but rather is to be understood as the "leading back" of a multiplicity to a "new" unity which comes from an original view that is characteristic of human beings. The "imagistic" root of the human world is that in it reality is "conveyed" or transformed into a new genus. The primacy of imagistic, directive, revelatory language lies in the fact that this is what makes deductions of any kind possible.

Landino distinguishes between "vulgar" and "original" poetry, the latter of which has metaphors rooted in what is primordial and "original." "[Poets] express deep and sublime feelings of the mind in elegant verses and are moved by a divine madness. . . . They often assert that wonderful things stand above our human powers, but as soon as this madness has dissipated, they are astonished at themselves. Therefore, they are those who Ennius rightly called the holy."[49]

This "fantastic induction" is all that is capable of ordering the human world and which has the power to rise to the position of leadership by revealing the direction for man to take.

> This is why the Latin people correctly called the poets "vates," from "vi mentis," i.e., because of the greatness of their thought and mind, and why the Greeks called the

"poetes" by the name "poieo" which means to create. . . .
They surpass all other writers, not only by their creativity in the ordering and structure of the "ornatus" but also
through the fame that they achieved among men. . . .
The moral philosophers did not yet exist when the divine
poet [Homer] showed us all the way to a good and happy
life and to the proper government of states and armies.[50]

Because poetry is rooted in "divine madness" there is an
identity between the poet and the theologian. Obviously the fact
that the poets "speak under a veil" and say the truth through
figmenta (which means that they use elements of the sensory
world in order to reach what transcends it and so to create the
world of the mind) is what brings forth the basic function of
poetry. Such a view implies rejecting the primacy of rational
speech in favor of the capacity of fantasy.

Now we are confronted with the problem that since work
and metaphor are the source of human history and society on
the humanistic view, we must determine from precisely what
area the humanists derived the rejection of rational thought that
conceives scientific thinking to proceed only from general and
necessary premises. Where, within Italian Humanism, is there a
"Copernican revolution" in the interpretations of scientific
method and language? This is the area of philology in the
translation of Greek texts into Latin. The work of the philolo-
gists proves to be that of the "dialectician," taken in the ancient
sense of the word. Aristotle, we should recall, defined dialectic
as the art of disputation in which—in contrast to the process of
scientific thought—*we do not begin with a first truth* in order to
prove something, *but from a specific, real "situation."*

Aristotle says that the advantages of such a dialectic are that
it provides exercise in discussion and is important for the
exchange of ideas because it helps us to locate the axioms and
starting points of the particular sciences. Here topics, as part of
dialectic, provides us with the different arguments that we need
in particular discussions. Topics is the doctrine of "finding"
[*invenire*] arguments. The aim of dialectic does not consist in the
provision of truth, but in providing that which can appear to be
true in a specific "situation" in time and space, the "probable"
[*verisimile*]. "Our work has the task of finding a method by
which we can form a conclusion from 'probable' statements for
every problem without coming to contradict ourselves."[51]

It was the humanist Leonardo Bruni (1369–1444) who came

to a fundamentally new idea on the basis of his efforts to translate anew Greek texts, especially the *Nicomachean Ethics.* Through the task of translating classical ancient texts, Leonardo Bruni became aware of the crisis of the philosophy of his time. He recognized that the texts from the philosophical tradition were in a pitiful condition; the translations were completely inadequate. Bruni complained that from Aristotle the scholastics "only took unpolished expressions so that they could insult the ear and bore the reader [*verba aspera, inepta dissona, quae cuiusvis aures obtundere ac fatigare possent*]."[52]

The task of translation led Bruni to the insight that the meaning of a term can be derived from the discovery of its sense only in the context of the relationships in which it stands. The meaning of a word, its different senses, is indicated by the arrangement or complex which contains it. This view is directly opposed to the rationalistic view that takes the meaning of a word to be fixed by its definition "in itself" and for which the concrete different relationships in which the word appears are considered to be mere coincidental accidents, completely without importance. However, it became clear to Bruni as a translator that a word carries different, changing meanings that can arise only in the context in which they appear. "All words are held in a fixed relationship to each other like a colored mosaic floor."[53]

Because the correct and thus "scientific" translation of a text can proceed only from the above-mentioned experience and insight, it follows that to begin with a priori, general meanings for terms in the interpretation of a text would be equivalent to doing violence to it and hence is "unscientific." This insight reveals a new concept of scientific thought and procedures.

The scientific structure of philology thus proves to be an aspect of dialectic, as Aristotle defined it, insofar as both begin with a particular situation—with the text for the philologist, with the discussion for the dialectician—in order to discover the sense of an expression.

In the interpretation of a text Bruni was forced to look for what lies at the bottom of it, i.e., the substance of its meaning, only in the framework of the whole context. This "whole" changes from one case to the next depending upon the texts. Each brings new concrete, individual meanings to terms that accordingly have to be understood in their changing senses.

With this Bruni goes beyond the limits of the problems of interpretation that we have been discussing. He recognizes further that language originates in the different situations in which human beings interact with reality. Since this interaction always occurs with regard to the achievement of a particular goal, so language can be effective only within a particular given historical time and a particular social situation. So the original source of the manifold meaning of an expression is to be found in its different uses [*usus*]. "*Usus ergo, qui tunc dominus fuit, etiam hodie dominus est. . . . Nos vero haec omnia variamus usu iubente.*"[34]

In this way an understanding of language is formed that is distinguished from rationalistic logic because it stresses the primacy of language's historical character, dialectic, and topics. From this it necessarily follows that "genuine" language is rhetorical, imagistic, and metaphorical, since this is the only kind that is formed with reference to the particularly confined state of the listener in time and space [*in optimo . . . scriptore . . . sit scribendi ornatus*].[35]

As far as the meaning and importance of the term *ornatus* is concerned, which we usually think of as "outer decoration," we should recall that *ornatus* originally came from the Greek term *Kosmos*, which refers in an ontological perspective to the "relationship" between particular parts and a whole and names the particular order that holds among them. The *ornatus*, therefore, is never something that belongs to particulars in isolation; only in relation to something else, a whole, does the particular receive its essential meaning and become part of an interconnected arrangement. Cicero uses *ornatus* in this original sense in reference to the reality of the world when he says: "Since in this one world the order of the relationships [*ornatus*] is so wonderful. . . ." Similarly he says in *De natura deorum*, "In this world there is great beauty and every order [*eximia pulchritudo sit atque omnis ornatus*]." Cicero uses this term in a political context as well, by remarking that "because the Athenians did not possess different grades of dignity, citizenship [*civitas*] did not retain its own order [*ornatum*]."[56]

Accordingly the source of "genuine" speech, as Bruni explained, is not reason [*ratio*] but a distinct capacity that is distinguished by the characteristics of "adaptability," "acuteness," and "momentariness."[57] Only *ingenium* is able to grasp [*coligere*] the relationship between things in a concrete situation in order to determine their meaning. This capacity has an "inventive" character, since it attains an insight without merely bringing out what is present in the premises as reason does in a

logical derivation. *Ingenium* reveals something "new" [*ingenio
. . . ad res novas proclives*], something "unexpected" and "as-
tonishing" by uncovering the "similar in the unsimilar," i.e.,
what cannot be deduced rationally.[58] With this definition Bruni
has determined the presupposition of all metaphorical thought
and speech.

Ingenium instead of reason, adaptable and acute speech
instead of rational speech, i.e., the *circumstantiae* are the original
source of our view of things. With this there is a complete
reversal of our interpretation of scientific thought. Rhetoric
suddenly has a new fundamental function.

What does the primacy of historical thought mean for the
rejection of the scientific model that defines reality on the basis
of unchanging first premises? Rhetorical and dialectical speech,
understood in Aristotle's sense, have in common that both
methods begin with temporally bound situations. It is only on
the basis of this procedure that they are able to "move" their
"listeners" and lead them to the action sought. On the other
hand there is a parallel between the grammarian—the philologist as an interpreter of a text—and the rhetorician insofar as
both begin with the insight that particular cases *are bound up in
a situation.* Since our historicity is characterized by the fact that
human beings always are confronted with decisions in the
context of tasks that arise "here" and "now," rhetorical language proves to be the only conclusive "genuine" language that
takes this fact into account.

In his *Suetoni expositio* Angelo Poliziano (1459–1494), who
calls himself a grammarian, not a philosopher, advances the view
that wisdom [*sapientia*] comes from the use of things [*sapientiam
. . . usus quidem genuit*]. Poliziano explains the meaning of this
thesis in his *Panepistemon,* where he mentions the different
ways in which human beings come to terms with nature so that
their world can come into being. Along with the traditional
"liberal" arts there are the "lower" [*sordidae*] arts like agricul-
ture, animal husbandry, and hunting that serve the fulfillment of
the immediate needs of life and because of their confinement to
times and places cannot be derived logically. Poliziano directs a
polemic attack against Plato as the representative of the primacy
of a priori thought: "A certain elder man in Athens denies that
the arts that essentially serve life rank as knowledge."[59] In his
lecture "Lamia" Poliziano rejects every philosopher who
"strives solely after the knowledge of that which always is,

always was, and exists beyond becoming." He emphasizes in his *Praelectio de dialectica* that the arts are especially useful "when they make the activity of the *ingenium* possible."[60]

With this the primacy of logical thought and language is broken, and rhetorical speech is ascertained to be the "genuine" form of language. "What is more wonderful than when we speak to the great mass of mankind so that we succeed in penetrating their soul and mind by giving their feelings a more gentle form through which we then rule the will and desire of all?"[61]

But whence does such a speech gain knowledge of that which is to be done? If rhetoric cannot provide an answer to this question, then it is reduced to mere sophistry. Here Poliziano stresses the essential importance of the example. In order to understand it in all of its ramifications, we must remember that, according to tradition, rhetoric is divided into three parts, the juristic, which treats of the past, the advisory, which is conducted with regard to the future, and, finally, the panegyric or eulogy which presents a measure or standard according to which the past and future can be evaluated. The panegyric presents what is exemplary and to which every judgment about men, actions, or situations must be referred. On the other hand it is possible to select human beings and their acts as exemplary models for the positive future only on the basis of precise knowledge of the present and past. This insight necessarily leads us to the primacy of historical thought, which achieves its true form in the three forms of rhetorical speech. Poliziano asks, "What is more lofty than to extoll and praise the people who excel in their capacities and deeds and to expose and destroy their opposite, the evil and disgraceful deeds?"[62]

In the changing "positions" in which man finds himself, that proves to be valid which lets his human existence develop and flourish. This happens within the frame of the three kinds of speech, the juristic, which orders the community through its constitutions, the political, through which the community's future is given form, and the panegyric. "All this served originally to bring the people who were in the fields within the walls of the city and to lead them to a common task. Whereas they previously went their own ways, these brought them together with laws, customs, and finally the culture of the city. This is why all well-ordered and civilized cities have flourished through the high art of speech." True wisdom, by which history develops, is the art of speech which now becomes the source of the "true" philosophy in place of the a priori deduction of the nature of reality.[63]

The Logic of Metaphor as Seeing the Similar

Work, metaphor, and the primacy of rhetorical speech—what kind of a new model for scientific thought and philosophizing do these three notions reveal? German Idealism denied that the metaphor has a philosophical importance. It only has a claim to a "lower" function in its relationship to thought because its task is restricted to preparing sense perceptions as a material for thought through the transferral of meanings, an original "untrue" form of understanding. Only with the *logos* do we achieve the "true" form of conceptual thought that is capable of grasping and presenting the essence of reality; the metaphor shows us reality in the form of its individual appearance. This material is taken over by the idea which reveals its deeper and true essence. Hegel's formulation reads: "When Spirit deepens its inner movement in the intuitive appearance of similar objects, it wants at the same time to free itself from their similarity. . . ."[64]

Hegel recognizes the metaphorical form of many logical expressions but stresses that these achieve a purely rational meaning only in the concept. " 'Comprehend', 'grasp', many words that have to do with cognition have a completely sensory meaning with reference to their actual meaning and this they thereby leave behind and exchange for a spiritual meaning; the first is sensory, the second spiritual."[65] For Hegel there is an *Aufhebung* of the metaphors which knowledge relies upon insofar as it transcends by reflection the immediate meaning of the images with which it begins. Through this transformation the metaphor receives the status of an "untrue" form, since it remains at the "lower" level of externalities which only mind is capable of grasping in its rational content.

For the Greeks the term "metaphor" originally signified a concrete activity, that of carrying an object from one place to another.[66] Later the term appeared in the context of language, when the meaning of a word was carried over from the physical to the mental sphere, as when the word "light" is taken to signify the source of insight.

In the classical tradition Aristotle often is referred to in this context. For him the metaphor is "correct transferral [*eu metapherein*], as a capacity to see the similar [*to homoion theorein*]."[67] It is the vision of the "common" that for Aristotle is the root of the fourfold form of the metaphor. "Transferral [*metapherein*] must be completed on the basis of similarity [*apo oikeion*] which, however, may not be too obvious."[68] The greater the "discovery" [*inventio*] of similarity is, the more surprising the metaphor itself seems to be. The ability to be metaphorical cannot be learned from another [*par allou labein*] because it stems as such from a gift [*euphuia*]. Yet the capacity to make these transfers is an original underived capacity that is a particularly effective method of teaching and learning. Metaphors bring things "immediately before our eyes" [*pro ommaton poiein*]. Their imagistic nature affects the passions, and this is why they are referred to the area of rhetoric. It must therefore be so constituted that through the discovery of relationships something peculiar and unique [*oikeion*] becomes obvious, "a unique feature [*oikeion*] . . . is to be conveyed."[69]

Furthermore Aristotle makes the decisive statement that rhetoric and philosophy arise from a common presupposition. "In philosophy too, it is characteristic of the one who accurately aims [*eustochos*] to see the similarity between things [*to homoion . . . theorein*] that are most distant from each other."[70]

The essential features of the metaphor are clarity [*to saphes*] insofar as their revelation must be univocal, that it awakens delight [*to hedu*] as a sign of successful intellectual work, and, finally, it is characterized by a unique strangeness [*to xenikon*] because it reveals something unusual and unexpected.

In *De oratore* Cicero discusses metaphors which he designates with the expressions *"translatio"* and *"quasi mutatio."* He defines them as the replacement of one expression by another [*"in alieno loco tamquam in suo positum"*]. He traces the use of metaphors to the following four reasons. First, it is a sign of intelligence to disregard that which is immediately obvious. Second, the listener enjoys learning while being led by metaphors. Third, it is pleasant to bear witness to a similarity on the basis of such a transfer of meaning. Fourth, because sight is the most active and sharpest sense, metaphor leads us to "see" something. "When someone expresses something with a figurative use of words that can only be signified with difficulty by the literal use of words then the similarity between the thing that we present in the figurative word and that which we want to make cognizable makes the latter intuitively clear [*illustrat id, quod intelligi volumus, eius rei, quam alieno verbo posuimus, similitudo*]." For this reason such metaphors are like loans, since something that we do not have is taken from somewhere else. Metaphors that do not imply a shortage are cleverer and lend a speech a certain "polish."[71]

According to Cicero the metaphor acts like a "light" because it presupposes an insight into "relationships." Since these relationships can be discovered in various phenomena, a metaphor is always possible. "There is really nothing in the nature of things whose word and concept we cannot also use in other regards [*nos non in aliis rebus possimus uti vocabulo et nomine*]. From wherever something is taken—and that is possible from everywhere—[*Unde enim simile duci potest—potest autem ex omnibus*] so a single similarity gives *light* to speech [*quod similitudinem continet*]."[72]

Cicero explains this idea with examples. We speak of "happy sowing" [*laetas segetes*]. Here the metaphor aims at revealing something that the literal word cannot immediately "show." Obviously sowing, viewed logically, is incapable of being either happy or sad. The metaphor, however, reveals the meaning that sowing holds *for people*. Furthermore Cicero defines the metaphor as an abbreviated comparison, for example, "when the shot escapes the hand [*si telum manu fugit*]." With the image of the "escape" the similarity between the shot and its meaning with regard to the human goal of action is "shown" in the briefest manner. Cicero remarks that finding [*inventio*] relationships is not accomplished by reason; "in this art [logic] . . . there is no prescription for how to find truth but only how it is to be evaluated or judged."[73]

We must return again to the beginning of our discussion. Language is divided into two fundamentally different forms of expression. One is purely rational, which serves to prove and provide the reasons for something. It is considered to be the measure of science, since it vouches for the objectivity of its statements with reasons, and these are not allowed to be clouded by subjective opinions. In ancient times this language was called "apodictic" insofar as it showed something [*deiknumi:* I show] upon [*apo*] the basis of reasons. It cannot be bound to times, places, or personalities; it is *unrhetorical*.

We said that proofs in this rational language must, in the traditional view, be free of metaphors because when words assume many meanings (and this is the presupposition of metaphorical speech) they prove to be imprecise. The final consequence of rational speech is the demand for a mathematical symbolic language in which consequences can be drawn from the premises that we assume. Because its "scientific" nature consists in its strictly deductive character, its essence is such that it can possess *no "inventive" character*. Such a language must restrict itself to finding what already is contained in the premises but not yet explicit or obvious.

The second form of language is the one that determines the premises themselves which, since they cannot be proven, are the *archai*, the principles. Now on the basis of what we have said about the metaphor and its characteristics by references to Aristotle and Cicero, we see that it and the language that is appropriate to metaphors have the characteristics of an "archaic" language. It is able only to make manifest and not to demonstrate. By virtue of its immediate structure this language "shows" us something, lets us see [*phainesthai*], and hence is "imagistic." Since it must rely upon images [*eide*] it has a "theoretical" [*theorein:* see or look at] character and yet has the metaphorical character that we have discussed. A meaning is conveyed [*metapherein*] to the "image" that is shown. By virtue of this fact it acts to give meaning.[74]

The metaphor, and hence the language which it draws upon, has an "archaic" character, "possesses principles," and is what we call "rhetorical." But this certainly is no longer understood as a mere technique for the "superficial" use of persuasion. Rather, on the basis of its archaic character, it is what outlines the basis or framework of rational argument; it comes "before" and provides that which deduction can never discover.

But how is this to be understood? Does metaphor lead exclusively to a poetic game, to a clever witty statement, as the Mannerists evidently believed?[75] Does ingenious activity—the viewing of unexpected relationships between sensory appearances—remain restricted to the field of the "aesthetic" so that it even leads man away from real tasks? In order to answer this question I want to go back one more time to the medieval tradition, but to the nonrational one which was somewhat concealed by the rationalistic one.

In the Middle Ages we find a theory of "seeing the similar" and the "simile" as the origin of human learning and culture. This can help us to bring out the background of our question more clearly. Hugo of St. Victor (1096–1141) represents a philosophical point of view that stands against the a priori logical philosophy of Paris and Oxford. Hugo begins with Pythagoras's doctrine that "similarity" is grasped in that which is similar [*"Pythagoricum namque dogma erat similia similibus comprehendere*"]. Hugo's basic thesis is: "We may not assume that the soul comes to receive similarity with all things from *somewhere else* or from *outside* [*neque enim haec rerum omnium similitudo aliunde aut extrinsecus animae advenire credenda est*] but rather it finds the distinction of like and unlike within and from itself [*in se et ex se*]."[76]

This means that the identification of similarity presupposes that its positive or negative importance for human life is revealed in the comparison of sensory phenomena with that which human self-realization requires. Only through this comparison do sensory phenomena acquire their meaning.

The origin of human cognition is analogical knowledge whereby the soul transfers meanings to appearances. "The soul, by grasping the similarity of things, returns to itself [*ad se ipsam rerum similitudines trahens aggregat*] and this is the cause of the fact that the mind itself, which grasps the universals, is composed of every substance and every being that it represents to itself."[77]

Here the universal, on the basis of which we define and recognize something, is *not* the product of a process of abstraction from previous insights but arises in the concrete comparison of phenomena with the principle of our own life itself. It is therefore a "commonness" of "similarity" that is ascertained concretely each time from case to case. Hugo calls the pursuit of knowledge a "going back to oneself" [*ad se ipsam retractatio atque advocatio*].[78]

In this way language assumes a decisive function for Hugo. It expresses the meaning of phenomena with regard to what the principle of life needs for its own realization from one instance to another. The meaning of the sensory phenomena, therefore, is *never* to be expressed or identified for all time. The basis of language is an insight, an *illuminatio* which uncovers the friendship [*amicitia*] between things and human beings [*videatur sapientiae studium . . . purae mentis illius amicitia*].[79] Hugo stresses that this *amicitia* arises through the use [*usus*] of things. For him the word cannot be separated from the confrontation resulting from different human needs.

I have gone back to this theory in order to show the sense in which "metaphor" lies at the base of human cognition and how this view stands in complete opposition to both purely formal theories of language and abstract theories that deduce the meaning of language in rationalistic terms from an a priori doctrine of being. We must understand the humanistic view of the primacy of metaphorical thought and language in just this way, that it has the characteristics of being "archaic," "original," "inventive," and "imagistic."

I said that the basic problem of logic is the connection or conjunction of the subject and that which is said about it or predicated of it. Traditional logic asserts the necessity of founding this "unity," whereby its problem is that of the proof, i.e., the derivation of a proposition from its premises. From this, we said, come the three aspects of logic, the concept, the definition, and the deductive derivation. Such a logic therefore proceeds from a concern to attain or reach what "is" and exists, since it is only by beginning with this that we can attain knowledge. Such a logic and form of language must pass over concrete reality.

A logic that holds "conveying meanings" and metaphor as the origin and basis of the interpretation of sensory phenomena is, in contrast to rational logic, a logic of images and metaphors. It will claim to be a logic of invention and not deduction. Like rational logic it will have to refer to concepts which, however, will have a completely different structure from rational concepts. That is, they will not "grasp" the real on the basis of a deductive process but rather on the basis of an immediate act or "view." As images such imagistic concepts would have the double role I have mentioned, to point out something and simultaneously to refer to something else because it is in this way that phenomena achieve a meaning. Put in another way the characteristic feature of an image is to convey a meaning. The image is a concept insofar as it presents a "relationship," a similarity, and so is a metaphorical concept. Such a logic is "fantastic" insofar as it shows a new world, that of humanity, and makes it open to view through metaphor.

The primacy of such a logic and ingenious imagistic language lies in the fact that it is only from this field that the meanings of phenomena can be conveyed with regard to their human connotation. In other words to "find" the point of comparison and similarity between reality and ourselves as human beings is to find the relationship needed to meet our material and spiritual needs. The concept as an image expresses this relationship immediately. Language, as Dante characterized it, evolves as question or answer ["*vel per modum interrogationis, vel per modum responsionis*"] in confrontation with material or spiritual needs.[80]

Inventive and metaphorical activity lies at the basis of

work, be it material or intellectual effort through which we strengthen our existence. Spiritual work consists in just this, that it answers the question of what the meaning of the "humanization" of nature is and hence what the meaning of work itself is. This twofold way of "conveying" things, this work, is the presupposition for the foundation of social and political institutions. It constitutes the premise of a "real" and not merely a "formal" calculus in reference to our own time. Such questions concern us, since the answers we give result in our way of existence. They are in no way "formal" questions that proceed from hypothetical premises and are not answered in such a context.

This "ingenious" metaphorical and fantastic activity is not realized in the framework of rational logic but in "common sense" [sensus communis] through which we continually transform reality in the human context by means of "fantastic" concepts. In such a language we never meet with abstract human beings but rather with those who, like ourselves, find themselves through work, in temporal and spatial relationships. The concepts through which we come to understand and "grasp" each situation come from our ingenious, metaphorical, fantastic capacities that convey meanings in the concrete situations with which we are confronted.[81]

In the basic sphere of our self-realization the forms by which we "convey" something prove to be the essential way in which reality is "humanized." This provides the necessity of commitment to fulfilling certain needs; directive images convey a meaning to reality characterized by urgency and interminability.

Fantastic universals have a primacy over abstract rational ones because concrete reality is revealed through them. For instance in Cicero's previously mentioned example the expression "happy sowing" is not rational and so not "scientific" in the traditional sense, but rather expresses the meaning which sowing has for human beings, a relationship (happy) which the supposedly "true" rational expression never would reveal. The same holds for the other example from Cicero, "when the shot escapes the hand." It aims at showing and revealing that which is really experienced and hence the concrete time in which human beings find things to receive a new meaning through work.

The conformity of reality to human needs comes about through human work, and this occurs through the conveyance of meaning in which fundamental metaphors reveal concrete reality, not in the frame of universal, abstract, rational language.

The insight and acuteness with which self-realization and the "humanization" of nature are connected is therefore fundamentally different from purely "literary," "playful" wit and acuteness. The wit by which the human world comes about carries out the engagement of our existence with the world on the basis of our freedom. It is this freedom from any kind of innate directive "images," "schemata," or "ideas" that is the basis of our strivings and historicity. This is the reason that man experiences himself to be unbounded in the face of nature. And it is not accidental that Dante saw the origin of different languages and human history in the loss of an existing "order." But it is in just this continuing experience of urgency that man's constant "attention" arises and the ties [*religio*] are discovered through which human effort is distinguished from that of animals, which also transforms reality, but only biologically. This original "tension" in which man lives and realizes himself is that through which attention is brought to the meaning of work. And man's attention to this tension illuminates the darkness of the manifold elements through which he constructs his "new" world.

The metaphorical imagistic form of language thus has attained a new meaning. It proves to be the only framework within which a new, neither rational and deductive nor formal manner of philosophizing can occur. Rhetorical language is primary and now acquires a philosophical importance whereby it realizes a new model of thought. This is the framework in which the humanistic tradition attains its contemporary theoretical importance.

Language as the Presupposition of Religion: A Problem of Rhetoric as Philosophy?

I must excuse myself in two ways regarding the title of this chapter and must ask for your forbearance. First of all, the title sounds unusual and even provocative, since the relationship of language and religion is—mildly put—unusual. Religiousness ordinarily is associated with inwardness and silence. The title thus sounds contradictory. Second, the subtitle, which is the claim to discuss the religious in the frame of rhetoric, is unusual. Under "rhetoric" we understand the general questions of communication. Are we here to discuss rhetoric in connection with the religious so that we are dealing with the question of rhetorical art in the sense of the art of preaching? My intention is a completely different one, namely—as it is formulated in the subtitle—a philosophical one. But it is precisely this which at first glance is not understandable. In the course of my considerations I hope to clarify the relationships that concern me here.

The Foundation for Immediacy in Sacred Symbols

The General Concept of Religion

Religion is defined as man's endeavor to construct a "holy and intact" cosmos which he conceives to be an overpowering reality other than himself. This reality is that to which man turns in order to give himself a place in an absolutely meaningful order. This occurs through reassurance in the form of rites.

Religiousness, defined this way, springs from the experience of the threat to man's being consumed by chaos and thus from the necessity of holding the terrible in check by giving reality a fixed meaning. The experience of anxiety before chaos appears again and again in history so that, should the justification of religion be proved, it reconfirms the view that the relevant knowledge of the man in the street, i.e., "common knowledge" and not theoretical constructions of the intellectuals, is decisive, *sensus communis.*

> The holy cosmos that surrounds man and encloses him in its order of reality, offers him the protection of the absolute against the greyness of the Anom. Whoever lives in the "right" relationship to the holy cosmos knows that he is protected against the nightmare of chaos. Whoever falls out of the "right" relationship to the holy cosmos bans himself to the border of meaninglessness.[1]

But with the pure "formal" insight with which religion claims to legitimize social institutions by giving them an ontologically valid status, it is certain that the justification of religion is not yet proven. It is perfectly clear that for a long time it has not fulfilled its function. Religion's claim is no longer recognized as the possibility for binding humanly defined existence to final, universal, holy reality in order to provide man's uncertain, short-lived constructions with security and permanence. If we note that theology is rooted in ritual and that the action of a ritual consists of things that must be done [*dromena*] and things that must be said [*legoumena*], then today we no longer have access to any valid ritual. Merely to give a "formal" definition of religion—namely, in regard to its role in society—without posing the questions *if* and *where* we still can speak of it meaningfully, circumvents the real problem.

The Characteristics of Sacred Language and Its Difference from Rational Speech

Since our starting point in the discussion of the problem of the religious is its relationship to language, we begin with the definition of sacred language—according to the previous definition of religion. Seen purely formally sacred language always has (*a*) a purely directive, revealing, or evangelical character (never a demonstrative or proving function), and it never arises out of a process of inference in order not to give up its original character or absolute undetermined character. (*b*) The statements of sacred language are formulated without any mediation, that is, "in the twinkling of an eye" and in an imagistic way. (*c*) They are "metaphorical" statements insofar as sacred language lends the reality of sensory appearances a new meaning. (*d*) The assertions of sacred language have a claim to urgency; the theoretical or practical view that does not fit with them is "outrageous." *(e)* Its announcements claim to stand outside of time.

Now the question emerges of *where and how*—in radical distinction to religious language—rational speech arises and wherein its different structure consists.

Rational speech, in explicit contradistinction to sacred speech, claims *(a)* to be demonstrative and to offer proof because it gives the reasons for its assertions. *(b)* Rational speech arises from a process of inference through which every form of immediateness and every metaphoric element is excluded. *(c)* Its statements have a purely formal character, and their validity depends exclusively on the premises to which they refer.

Today's situation is such that in our desacralized and demythologized world we believe in no annunciations, in no purely directive statements, in no evangelist, be it a God or a prophet. We turn to rational thought, to proofs and reasons in order to free ourselves from the subjectivity and relativity of appearances. It is useless to go to the "evidence" of original premises, to their "analysis," in order to escape the circle of rational speech and thought. Reliance on the evidence of "first" premises cannot escape the criticism of relativity and subjective psychologism. Hence we have the frequent priority of "formal" logic, "formal" semiotic, and structuralist linguistics. Thus not only is every access to religious sacred texts closed to us but so also is the possibility of a metaphysics, a science that tells us about the "essence of man" (Humanism).

The Immediate Nonverbal Code in the Biological Code

Is there an area we can point to in which we are able to find purely "directive," "compelling," "figurative" signs standing "outside of time" that instantly give meaning? In order to enter into this question we first want to leave the world of *logos* and language and to refer to the organic world.

In the realm of the organic *(a)* every genus and species of life stands under the signs that are governing and directive for it—"codes" we call them today. By means of these codes living creatures decipher reality and bind it to the fixed order of their environment. Sounds, movements, smells, and colors receive an immediate "directive function." Aristotle speaks of "directive sounds" [*psophoi semantikoi*].[2] These directive signs are proper to life for the completion of such different functions as nutrition, reproduction, and flight from danger. *(b)* According to what was just said, reality appears to the living creature exclusively within selections [*diastema*], that is, within the frame of the "code" on the basis of which reality can be deciphered meaningfully. The basic function of life appears as something "metaphorical"; the "environment" of the organic, which is not identical with reality, arises out of the lending of meanings for life and is composed of such meanings. If fantasy is defined as the activity of "letting appear" [*phainesthai*], then we must admit that through the organic's power to lend meaning, it therefore has a kind of fantasy and every genus and species has one of its own; it is what determines its environment. *(c)* On the organic level there is an unbroken unity of those signs that are meaningful for life. This unbroken unity of directions and actions forms the "symbolic functional circle of life" (Jacob von Üxküll). This is symbolic [*sumballein:* unite] insofar as the directive signs [*semata*] and the actions they bring about stand in the frame of needs of life that are to be satisfied and only receive their meaning for life within this context.

In this biological functional circle there is neither a continuity of the objects of life—because these never exist "in themselves" and cannot be abstracted from the rhythm of life—nor a holding at a distance or separation of subject and object, since both of these stand in an unbroken unity, in an immediate relationship.

(d) We speak of "induction" in the original sense of this expression [*ep-agein, in-ducere*], that is, as the "tracing back of something to something else" and find that in organic life there arises in its symbolic functional circle the inductive power of original directive signs. These "lead" that which the organs reveal back to that which is indispensable for life. Allow me just one example from zoology. Ticks are blind and deaf. They react only to a certain smell, that of butyric acid. This "sign" [*sema*] brings two actions into play; the tick falls onto its prey and bores into it in order to feed. It has been proved that the tick has no sense of taste (it sucks only that which shows a certain smell and particular temperature, even when the prey is not warmblooded). Moreover, it is able to wait up to eighteen years for this moment. The zoologist Jacob von Üxküll has referred to this action as a hangman's mealtime, for after that nothing is left for it but to drop to the ground in order to lay its eggs and die. The whole of reality "collapses" here to a few "directive" signs, smell and touch and the actions appropriate to them.

You will ask what these comments on the various aspects of

the organic are for, that have nothing in common with the problem of the religious or of the rhetorical. We notice with surprise, however, that all of those aspects that we mentioned can be found in the sacred world. *(a)* The signs that govern here "direct," "command," and "necessitate" the living creature to certain actions that are always identical. Because of this analogy with the sacred world, we can speak of "ritual" with animals in different scenes of life. *(b)* These signs possess a metaphorical function for they transfer a meaning to what the organs announce. By means of this lending of meanings every organism's specific environment appears to it, which for it is the only reality. *(c)* The signs have an inductive "leading" character. *(d)* The development of these environments, these *kosmoi*—in the double sense of the Greek expression as order and as decoration—occurs on the organic level not for the sake of the life of the particular individual but rather for the preservation of the species. It also is not just the particular living creature, that is, the individual that accomplishes this transference of meanings because it takes place through signs that belong to the species. *(e)* Finally on the basis of the immediately directive signs that govern the organic sphere, we perceive a strictly nonverbal kind of communication and understanding. The signs, be they colors, sounds, smells, or movements, present an immediate meaning.

It is certainly no coincidence that, by means of the definitive aspects of the sacred and their parallelism with the organic, the Greeks joined to celebrate the cycle of the organic in cults like those of Demeter.

The Forming of a Human Order through Rhetorical Speech

The Rupture of the Immediate Nonverbal Code: Human Anxiety

The problem is, through what does the human world arise if man, in distinction to animals, has no immediate environment, if this must be constructed again and again by the individual? In other words what is the cause of the "humanization" of nature? The second essential question is, how does this construction of the human world stand in relationship to the phenomenon of language, of *logos*? Third, is it possible, and if so, *how* can we overcome the purely "formal" conception of knowledge that controls today's conception of science? But this question stands in the closest relationship to the problem of religion. We can connect these three questions in this way: *Where* and *how* does the unharmed and holistic world of the organic disappear on the anthropological level?

On the anthropological level there is no longer a unity of the symbolic functional circle in which the subject and object are narrowly bound by the organic that appears and recedes according to the various scenes of life's functions. At this level sensory appearances are constituted as objects that the subject acts to define in their meanings. In place of the immediate "phonetic" communication—as in the zoological world—there appears in the anthropological sphere the task of giving sensory appearances names in order to define them through reasons [*legein*] in speech, i.e., through a rational process. This is *logos* instead of *psophos semantikos* according to the Aristotelian definition. No inductive power is here at work but rather induction is "logical" in that a unity is abstracted from a manifold.

With the word [*logos*] and the giving of names, the sense object is isolated. It appears as something existing in abstraction and held at a distance in "objectivization"; that is, it appears as a continuum that is not present at the organic level. Fantasy, as the capacity to lend meanings, is left to the individual; on the basis of man's tasks he emerges for the first time as an individual. The individual human being and not the immediate directive signs of the holistic and unproblematic world has the task of constructing the world that is lived in.

With this splitting up of the unity of subject and object (unlike that in the symbolic functional circle of the organic) men suffer "anxiety" when standing before possibilities, the anxiety that arises in the basic experience of not having available an immediately effective code. Kierkegaard says: "Anxiety is the reality of freedom as the possibility for possibility. Therefore we cannot find 'anxiety' in animals, simply because they are not defined in their naturalness as spirit or mind." From this Kierkegaard concludes that whoever is "educated" through anxiety, "is educated through possibility."[3]

Obviously "education" and "spirituality" in their original sense do not point to rational knowledge. The meaning of anxiety as the possibility of freedom certainly lies in the fundamental experience that no immediate code for deciphering the real is available to human beings so that they can define their environment.

On the biological level anxiety does not arise (which is why

Kierkegaard asserts that animals are happy and satisfied because they have no capacity for intelligent thought). Anxiety comes from the loss of a code within which life objects and subjects appear. The animal is not in danger of being set outside of the code that is valid for it. The difference between the biological and anthropological situation is defined by a fixed code in the frame of which "directive" signs are decisive.

The Problem of the Function of Language

The principal question now is directed to the definition of the ground of the human "situation" through which the rise of *logos*, the word, is brought into play in place of the directive expression, the *phone semantike*. The problem is whether there is actually a governing code for human beings, and if so, how it actually takes effect and how it is structured. Here it is important to determine that the problem of the religious then can be discussed only in the frame of the problem of language and, to be specific, as the question of the cause of the collapse of the unity of the symbolic functional circle of life.

There are two reasons that can be taken into consideration as the basis of the collapse of the symbolic functional circle of life. First, language itself is the truest cause of the dissolution of the unity of the organic insofar as it abstracts and isolates the objects of life from that rhythm of life in which they arise and receive their particular meaning.

As an example I want to mention two different representatives of this thesis. It has been noted by Thure von Üxküll that the child first learns its human code from the mother who in turn has learned it as language from the series of generations of a culture: "The mother, by translating the preverbal dialogue into a verbal one, helps the child finally to construct objects and an ego that opposes the objects out of the sensations that at first just overwhelm it."[4]

The French morphologist René Thom has formulated an analogous thesis. He compares organic with anthropological life and says:

> The psychic life of animals is always under the influence of certain automechanisms . . . that are closely bound up with the perception of biologically important objects like predators and prey. . . . When a predator (B) identifies itself with the prey (A), it is easy to see that an "index"

of A ipso facto proves itself as an index of B. . . . On the basis of this fascination that objects hold, the "ego" of the animal is *no permanent entity*. Accordingly, the distinction between subject and object does not exist in a permanent way for it.[5]

In contrast to this biological situation Thom stresses the human being:

> In the development of the child it is well known that the period of the first to third years of life is critical; when the child does not hear its own parents speak during this stretch of time, the learning of language and the intellectual development are irreparably compromised. . . . It can be assumed that the child undergoes a fundamental alienation from certain living things and objects that effect a total fascination on it. . . . The fascination of things is then gone from the human psyche; we can assume that the symbolic activity and the appearance of language here plays a decisive role in this revolution. . . . In this way human language allows the depiction of a distant (in time and space) process and liberates the mind from the tyranny of the "hic et nunc" to which the animal is bound.[6]

According to this interpretation an "isolation" of objects is attributed to fantasy; fantasy imagines an "inner" subjective and an "outer" objective world through which the abstraction of an "inner" and an "outer" arises and hence the duality of the subject and object.

The Basic Power that Leads to the Breaking of the Immediate Nonverbal Code by Means of the Word

Against the view explained previously that the basis of the dissolution of the immediate functional circle of life is language, it should be noted that only when the original unity of subject and object has been "broken through," and hence the preverbal phonetic possibility of communication has disappeared, can the task of the definition of isolated appearances arise in order that this unity can be created anew.

Why should human beings otherwise seek and assert the word [*logos*] as an element of "another" code in place of the preverbal? Only when the *phone* as a directive expression [*semantikos psophos*] has sunk to a pure *psophos*, that is, to a sound that no longer carries meaning, does the necessity of a "new" form of defining through the word [*logos*] arise, that is, by linguistic communication.

The meaningful function of language can be explained only as the overcoming of the rise of "isolation," "abstraction," and the separating out of subject and object. The necessity of a verbal definition thus urges itself upon us then, when "preverbal" communication has become weak. Language is not the *cause* of the separating out of the duality of subject and object but rather the result of it, with the task of reconstructing the broken unity in a *new* way. The insufficiency of the preverbal "code" is the immediate presupposition of the function of language, for here we are confronted with the distinctly human phenomenon of the absence of an immediate code. Through the word the attempt is undertaken to bridge the isolation of the objects of life from the subject. The task of language consists in finding and forming a *sumploke,* a connection of the subject and object through the verb.

If the insufficiency of the biological code were something like the result of a loss of the function of life (a first reason for the clarification of the function of language), then the word only would be to explain the result of what in the field of zoology is called a "domestication phenomenon," i.e., as a letting up of the power of life. With this, however, language as such and all of the historical works of the "spirit," such as art, technology, and science, would be mere indications of the disappearance of life.

We must counter this kind of domestication, understood as "alienation" from the original unity of the function of life. Should this interpretation of the reason for the insufficiency of the biological code prove to be untenable, then it would be understandable only as the entry of a power that dissolves the unity of the symbolic function of life, a power whose hidden and yet effective strength is that upon which the origin of a new "code"—the human code—and world depend. Through this human "spirituality" life receives a completely different meaning compared to the biological world.

Anxiety, as the experience of standing before possibilities and having to choose between them, points to a necessity, the experience of which has a cathartic function. Here we should note the following: In connection with the problem of anxiety Freud identified the "domestic" character of human beings with animistic views, with narcissistic views of the self, with sexual fantasies which become causes of anxiety when suppressed.[7] The problem consists, however, in the question of whether anxiety does not point primarily to the basic existential experience of the insufficiency of the biological code. In the last analysis it has to do with the experience of the basic power that leads to the breaking through from the purely biological functional circle, and that, by means of the word, leads men to the cognition of that power, i.e., to consciousness of their own "strange and nondomesticated" situation.

The experience of the necessity of a process of legitimation arises from language, that is, the search for the proper "place" in a new system of relations in which man defends and maintains his original reality: this is the problem of religiousness. It is important in this context to recall Emanuel Swedenborg's thesis that "in the most inner meaning of the word, the only subject is the Lord, and all instances of the glorification of his humanness are described by the word. . . . The Lord alone is in the innermost of the word."[8]

The Mirror of the Word

I already have mentioned Kierkegaard, and in this context I want to make it clear that in order to be read correctly Kierkegaard, too, must have his views "turned around." In his work *A Self-Examination That Is Recommended to Everybody*, which in the Italian translation E. Castelli rightly entitles *The Mirror of the Word,*[9] he tells us how we are to read a text that for him counts as holy (the Old and New Testaments). The evangelical word must be read again and again just as though it were directed to us personally—that is, subjectively—in order to make us responsible. Since we no longer recognize the mythic word of God, Kierkegaard's work no longer concerns us so that from this point of view it seems to have a meaning only for Christians.

But if we recognize that in the word is revealed that which breaks through the symbolic functional circle of biological life, i.e., that which releases the power of inductive signs that are effective here, then Kierkegaard's text, his appeal to "see ourselves in the text,"[10] receives a completely new meaning. We see ourselves in "the mirror of the word" in order to see or "find" a "new" world in and through it. "That is what we most of all must achieve in the mirror of the word; we must not look into the mirror but into ourselves."[11]

"To see us in the mirror of the word," it is the word that breaks out and flames up in us to order appearances in its light.

It is the word "suffered" as a necessity and experienced as a command that we live through in our desperation and doubt and which presents us "directly" to the new. It does not concern the word as it already is found in a mythic text and that only has to be interpreted in an existential sense because for us there are no longer any "holy" texts. The only text that is evangelical for us is the live urgency of the word. Kierkegaard's statement must be read in the sense that "the word directs itself to me, it concerns me," for only in it can I find myself again in that I recover my world from nature. Kierkegaard's frightening admission is that "I do not yet quite dare to be completely alone with the word, in a solitude in which no illusions intrude."[12]

The loneliness in the word means loneliness with himself in order to let the "new" world appear; how difficult it is with all our care, with all our anxiety, with all of our repulsion, and with our whole consciousness "to submit to the power of the word." In this sense we maintain with Kierkegaard that "our fathers heard the frightful voice of the word, but today it sounds so objective, so abstract, as if it came to us through cotton wool insulation."[13]

If the reader of magic formulas can conjure up spirits—so Kierkegaard wrote—"so you must yourself experience fear and trembling in your soul, and only thus . . . will you achieve being a human being, a personality, that is free from the absurdity that we are the unpersonal 'objective' creatures that we have become."[14]

The Preeminence of Rhetorical Language

Until now I have referred to the word [*logos*] as the source of the human world, the world as an expression of desperation in the specifically human situation, in order to create an order in the midst of the chaos of sensory impressions. The question that must be posed here, however, is the following: What word [*logos*] concerns us here? We distinguish fundamentally in language [*logos*] between the word as a name [*onoma*] and as a verb [*rhema*]. This distinction points to a fundamental meaning. The word as a noun is a designation of that which we call the object [*objectum*]. But an object never exists in isolation, since it always appears only in the dynamics of a task to be fulfilled with regard to certain needs. Since, at the same time, this task occurs in the frame of the not yet, no more, or now, i.e., in the frame of the time span, the word [*logos*] stands as a name [*onoma*] in a concrete statement [*legein*] only in connection with the verb [*rhema*]. This means that the word only occurs in the area of a concretely active task that is to be carried out and never has validity as an expression of an abstract isolated object.

This insight proves once again how the word is in no way that which isolates and abstracts sensory appearances. These appear to us as objects, in the concrete urgency of life, to be given a meaning in order to incorporate them in the context of a task in some particular cosmos.

The word as the presupposition and announcement of the religious thus is expressed in rhetorical language, in that language that urges itself on us in our desperate and pathetic engagement, for with it the chief concern is the formation of human existence.

Thus we have a threefold human connection: on the one hand of language with the experience of the religious; then the experience of the religious with *pathos* (but not with the rational word); and finally the relationship between rhetorical speech and the philosophical problem of the definition of the essence of man, for only in this last connection does the basis and the whole range of rhetorical speech present itself. Let us not forget, as Dante asserted in *De vulgari eloquentia,* that the origin of language is question and answer [*"vel per modum inter-rogationis, vel per modum responsionis"*].[15] The whole range of this discussion must be supplemented by the following consideration: Rational speech is that which strictly, "mathematically" explains or "infers" what is implied in the premises. This speech is "monological" in its deepest structure, for it is not bothered by emotion or place and time determinations in its rational process; it follows the ideal of philosophizing that Descartes created for us.

Rhetorical speech on the other hand is a "dialogue," that is, that which breaks out with vehemence in the urgency of the particular human situation and "here" and "now" begins to form a specifically human order in the confrontation with other human beings. And because the material belonging to language consists in the interpretation of the meaning of sensory appearances—for the main thing is to order and form these—it is laden with figurative expressions, color, sounds, smells, tangibles. It proves in the highest degree to be "metaphoric" speech, laden with symbols in accordance with a formulation of Baudelaire's. "Nature is a temple in which living pillars sometimes let forth confused words; man passes therein through a wood of symbols. They give him familiar views like wide echoes, that are prolonged in the distance in a deep and dark unity like the night and the brightness, mix and respond to the smells, colors, and sounds."[16]

Everywhere today semiotics is mentioned. It is supposed to be the doctrine of the signs [semata] that open the meaning of sensory appearances; we find it in linguistics, rhetoric, and the history of literature. If such a doctrine is not to degenerate into a pure formalism, it must be able to rise to the level of philosophy, as the doctrine of signs on the basis of which specifically human work [ergon anthropinon] appears. This means a philosophical task that proceeds to the question of the origin of human language. It means a principal rejection of formal semiotics, strict linguistics, and rhetoric understood only as an art of persuasion.

Notes

Chapter 1

1. Bertrando Spaventa, *La filosofia italiana nelle sue relazioni colla filosofia europea* (Bari, 1908).

2. Ibid., p. 31.

3. Ibid., pp. 193-94. Cf. Ernesto Grassi, *Vom Vorrang des Logos. Das Problem der Antike in der Auseinandersetzung zwischen italienischer und deutscher Philosophie* (Munich, 1939).

4. G. W. F. Hegel, *Vorlesungen über die Geschichte der Philosophie, Sämtliche Werke: Jubilämsausgabe,* 20 vols., ed. Hermann Glockner (Stuttgart: Frommann Verlag, 1928), 17:126.

5. Ibid., p. 20.

6. Carl Prantl, *Geschichte der Logik* (Leipzig, 1855), p. 522; Theodor Mommsen, *Römische Geschichte* (Berlin: 1933), p. 117; "M. Tullius Cicero," in A. Pauly and G. Wissowa, *Real-Encyclopädie der classischen Altertumswissenschaft* (Stuttgart: J. B. Metzler, 1939), pp. 1189-90.

7. Ernesto Grassi, "Der Beginn des modernen Denkens," in *Jahrbuch der geistigen Überlieferung,* Band 1, Berlin, 1940.

8. Ludwig Wittgenstein, *Tractatus logico-philosophicus,* trans. C. K. Ogden (London: Routledge and Kegan Paul, 1933).

9. *Tractatus* 5. 472.

10. Giambattista Vico, *The New Science of Giambattista Vico,* trans. Thomas Goddard Bergin and Max Harold Fisch (Ithaca: Cornell University Press, 1968), par. 331.

11. Ibid., par. 1106.

12. Ibid., par. 375 and 34.

13. "Orazione in Morte di Donna Angela Cimmino Marchesa di Petrella," *Opere di G. B. Vico,* ed. Fausto Nicolini, 8 vols. in 11 (Bari: Laterza, 1911-1941), 7:170.

14. Ernesto Grassi, *Humanismus und Marxismus. Zur Kritik der Verselbständigung von Wissenschaft* (Hamburg, 1973).

15. Cicero *De finibus* 5. 15, 41; *De inventione* 1. 2.

16. Cicero *De legibus* 1. 33; *De finibus* 1. 18; *De oratore* 3. 29, 160; *Topica* 1. 38; *Tusculanae Disputationes* 3. 2.

17. Cicero *De inventione* 1. 30, 49; *Oratio pro A. Caecina* 5.

18. Cicero *Topica* 2. 6; *De oratore* 2. 38, 157.

19. Cicero *De oratore* 2. 56, 230; *De legibus* 1. 26; *De oratore* 3. 16, 61.

20. Cicero *De re publica* 1. 2; *De officiis* 1. 153; *De oratore* 1. 47.

21. Cicero *De inventione* 1. 2; *Topica* 1. 76, 70.

22. Ernesto Grassi, *Macht des Bildes: Ohnmacht der rationalen Sprache. Zur Rettung des Rhetorischen* (Cologne: DuMont, 1970); cf. *Humanismus und Marxismus.*

23. The *Fabula de homine* is available in English translation by Nancy Lenkeith along with other writings of Renaissance humanists in *The Renaissance Philosophy of Man,* ed. Ernst Cassirer, Paul Oskar Kristeller, and John Herman Randall, Jr. (Chicago: University of Chicago Press, 1948), pp. 387-93. The following quotations refer to this English edition. Other citations refer to Vives, *Opera omnia,* 8 vols. (Valencia, 1782-1790).

24. *A Fable about Man,* p. 390; *Opera,* tom. 4, pp. 3-9.

25. *A Fable about Man,* p. 390.

26. Cf. Boccaccio, *Genealogia deorum;* Coluccio Salutati, *De laboribus Herculis.*

27. *A Fable about Man,* p. 389; *Opera,* tom. 4, p. 5.

28. *A Fable about Man,* p. 390; *Opera,* tom. 4, p. 6.

29. *A Fable about Man,* p. 390; *Opera,* tom. 4, p. 7.

30. J. L. Vives, *De disciplinis,* Liber 4, quid est de corrupta rhetorica; *Opera,* tom. 6, p. 152.

31. *De disciplinis,* p. 152.

32. Ibid., pp. 8-9.

33. Ibid., p. 8; J. L. Vives, *De ratione dicendi, Opera,* tom. 2., p. 153.

34. See J. W. Hoffmann, *Etymologisches Wörterbuch des Griechischen* (Munich, 1950), p. 22; A. W. Walde, *Lateinisches etymologisches Wörterbuch* (Heidelberg 1938),1:66.

35. Emmanuele Tesauro, *Il Cannocchiale Aristotelico, ossia Idea dell' arguta e ingegnosa elocuzione, che serve a tutta l'Arte oratoria lapidaria e simbolica* (Venice, 1670), pp. 47 and 70.

36. Ibid., p. 500.

37. Tesauro, *La Filosofia Morale* (Turin, 1670), pp. 241-42.

38. Tesauro, *Il Cannocchiale Aristotelico,* p. 112.

39. Ibid.

40. Giovanni Pellegrini, *Delle Acutezze* (Genoa, 1639), pp. 32 and 45.

41. Ibid., p. 40. "Ha luogo solamente e principalmente non già nel provare . . . ma nel *farle,*" in Pellegrini, p. 42.

42. Baltasar Gracián, *Agudeza y Arte de Ingenio, Obras completas* (Madrid, 1967), p. 236.

43. Ibid., pp. 241a-241b.

44. Gracián, *El Heroe, Obras completas,* S., 9b.

45. Ibid.

Chapter 2

1. *An Essay Concerning Human Understanding,* 2 vols., ed. Alexander Campbell Fraser (Oxford: Clarendon Press, 1894), vol. 2, bk, 3, ch. 10, sec. 34.

2. *The Critique of Judgement: Part I, Critique of Aesthetic Judgement,* trans. James Creed Meredith (Oxford: Clarendon Press, 1952), sec. 53.

Chapter 3

1. See E. Grassi, *Macht des Bildes: Humanismus und Marxismus,* pp. 74-256; "Rhetoric and Philosophy," in *Philosophy and Rhetoric* 9, no. 4 (1976); *Kunst und Mythos* (Hamburg, 1957), pp. 107-43; "Marxism, Humanism and the Problem of Imagination in Vico's Works," in *G. B. Vico's Science of Humanity,* ed. G. Tagliacozzo and D. Verene (Baltimore: Johns Hopkins University Press, 1973); "Der Beginn des modernen Denkens," pp. 36-85.

2. See B. Spaventa, *La filosofia italiana,* pp. 30ff; Hegel, *Geschichte der Philosophie,* 19:328.

3. E. Cassirer, *Das Erkenntnisproblem* (Berlin, 1922). In regard to an opposite criticism of Humanism, see E. Kessler, "Das Problem des frühen Humanismus," in *Humanistische Bibliothek* (Munich, 1968), vol. 1.

4. Descartes, *Regulae ad directionem ingenii,* Rule 4, in *Oeuvres,* ed. C. Adam and P. Tannery (Paris, 1908), 10:371.

5. Descartes, *Discours,* pt. 1, p. 14.

6. See P. Bracciolini, "Epistulae," in Muratori, *Rerum italicarum scriptores,* 20:160.

7. Descartes, *Discours,* pt. 1, p. 9.

8. Descartes, *Regulae ad directionem ingenii,* Rule 3, p. 366.

9. Vico, *De nostri temporis studiorum ratione,* chap. 3.

10. Ibid.

11. Ibid.

12. Ibid., chap. 7.

13. Ibid., chap. 3.

14. Ibid.

15. Aristotle *Topica* 100a 18ff.

16. Ibid., 101a 29ff.

17. Ibid., 101b 13.

18. Cicero *De oratore* 2. 36, 152.

19. Tacitus *Dialogus de oratoribus* 31.

20. Cicero *Topica* 2, 7.

21. Ibid., 2, 6; see also *De oratore* 2. 32, 137ff. and 2. 38, 157; Quintilian *Inst. orat.* 5. 10, 20 and 12. 2, 13.

22. Boethius, *Opera* (Basel, 1570), p. 827.

23. Quintilian *Inst. orat.* 3. 5, 1; Cicero *De oratore* 1. 31, 142; see also the division with Quintilian *Inst. orat.* 3. 3, 1.

24. Vico, *De studiorum ratione,* chap. 3.

25. Vico, *Opere,* ed. Gentile and Nicolini (Bari, 1914), 1:271.

26. Vico, *Scienza nuova, Opere,* p. 213.

27. Vico, "Giornale dei letterati," in *Opere,* 1:212; Vico, *De*

antiquissima Italorum sapientia, 1:7, 4. One of the causes which hinder us from recognizing the philosophical importance of topics that Vico maintains lies in the traditional schematization of this concept. This misunderstanding is still visible, e.g., in E. R. Curtius's work *Europäische Literatur und lateinisches Mittelalter* (Berne, 1948).

28. Quintilian *Inst. orat.* 3. 3, 1.
29. Ibid., 1. 4.
30. Ibid., 1. 5.
31. Ibid., 1. 13.
32. Ibid., 1. 13-14.
33. Ibid., 3. 3, 1; 8. 6.
34. Ibid., 2. 21, 4; 3. 6, 1-5.
35. A little further he repeats the same idea. Ibid., 3. 6, 21.
36. Ibid., 3. 6, 23-24.
37. Ibid., 3. 6, 80-81.
38. Ibid., 3. 11, 1.
39. Ibid., 1. 4, 2.
40. Ibid., 1. 4, 18; 1. 5, 2; see also Horace *Ars poetica* v. 311.
41. Quintilian 2. 4, 7. See Machiavelli, *Principe,* chap. 6, 25, 26.
42. Poliziano, *Oratio super Fabio Quintiliano et Statii Sylvis, Opera omnia* (Lugduni, 1553), 3:107-8. Poliziano demands recognition for his deed to have brought again the ancient authors to their proper place and honor. He praises himself for having brought to the ancient texts in the libraries the right of residency. See Poliziano, p. 108.
43. Poliziano, "Lamia," in *Le Selve e la Strega,* ed. I. Del Lungo (Florence, 1925), p. 24.
44. Poliziano, Letter to Lorenzo Medici in *Epistolarium,* 12:445-46.
45. Poliziano, "Lamia," p. 26.
46. Ibid., p. 27.
47. See Quintilian *Inst. orat.* 2. 4, 18; 1. 4, 2; 1. 5, 2.
48. Poliziano, *Or. super Quint. et Stat.,* pp. 111-12.
49. Ibid., p. 111.
50. Giovanni Pico della Mirandola, *De genere dicendi philosophorum,* in E. Garin, *Prosatori Latini del Quattrocento* (Naples, 1952), pp. 804-22; E. Barbaro, *Epistulae, Orationes et Carmina,* ed. V. Branca (Florence, 1943), pp. 84-87.
51. Barbaro, p. 86.
52. Ibid.
53. G. Pico, *De genere dicendi philosophorum,* p. 806.
54. Ibid., p. 808.
55. Ibid., p. 818.
56. Ibid., p. 808.
57. Ibid., p. 810.
58. Ibid., p. 808.
59. Ibid., p. 820.

60. Ibid., p. 804.
61. Ibid., p. 806.
62. Ibid.
63. Ibid.
64. Ibid., p. 808.
65. Ibid., p. 812.
66. Ibid., p. 814.
67. Ibid.
68. Ibid., p. 816.
69. Ibid. See also p. 820.
70. Gianfrancesco Pico, *De imaginatione*, chap. 1, p. 24. I am quoting from the edition by H. Caplan, *G. F. Pico, On the Imagination. The Latin Text with an Introduction, an English Translation and Notes* (New Haven, 1930).
71. Ibid.; see also W. Raith, "Die Macht des Bildes. Ein humanistisches Problem bei G. F. Pico della Mirandola," in *Humanistische Bibliothek* (Munich, 1968), vol. 3. In regard to the problem of imagination, see W. Szilasi, *Phantasie und Erkenntnis* (Berne, 1969).
72. Ibid.
73. G. F. Pico, *De imaginatione*, chap. 5, p. 38.
74. Ibid., chap. 6, p. 40.
75. See W. Raith, "Die Macht des Bildes."
76. G. F. Pico, *De imaginatione*, chap. 10, pp. 62ff.
77. G. F. Pico, *Examen vanitatis doctrinae gentium*, *Opera* (Basel, 1573), p. 1006.
78. G. F. Pico, *De fide et ordine credenda theoremata*, *Opera* (Basel, 1573), p. 253.
79. Grassi, "Rhetoric and Philosophy."
80. K. Kosik, *Die Dialektik des Konkreten* (Frankfort/M., 1967), p. 7.

Chapter 4

1. Aristotle *Metaphysics* 1054 b 7.
2. John Scotus, *De Divisione Naturae*, 5.4.
3. Ibid., 3.27.
4. Peter Abelard, "Glossulae super Porphirium" in *Schriften* (Münster, 1933), 2:505.
5. Descartes, *Discourse on Method*, pt. 2, p. 11. Cf. pt. 1, p. 10.
6. Johann Gottlieb Fichte, "Über den Begriff der Wissenschaftslehre (1794)," in *Sämtliche Werke*, ed. J. H. Fichte (Berlin: Veit, 1845), 1:53; G.W.F. Hegel, *Vorlesungen über die Geschichte der Philosophie*, 19:328; 17:121.
7. Brunetto Latini, *Li livres dou Tresor*, ed. F. J. Carmondy (Berkeley: University of California Press, 1949), p. 21.
8. Ibid., pp. 327-28.
9. Ibid., p. 318.
10. Cicero *De inventione* 1. 2, 88-89.

11. Giambattista Vico, *The New Science.*
12. Cicero *Pro archia* 18; bk. 1, vol. 2, pp. 791-92.
13. Ibid., 27; vol. 1, p. 794.
14. Horace *Ars Poetica* 5.391ff.
15. Ibid., 5. 403ff.
16. Ibid., 5. 312ff.
17. Dante, *De vulgari eloquentia,* German translation by F. Dornseiff and J. Balogh (Darmstadt, 1965), bk. 2. See Dante, *Purgatorio,* canto 32, line 69; *De monarchia,* 2, 12. 7; 3, 4. 16.
18. Dante, *Convivio* (Torino: Loescher, 1968), 3, 4. 1; 1, 10. 13; 1, 7. 14; 4, 6. 4.
19. Dante, *De vulg. eloq.* 1, 4. 4.
20. Ibid., 1, 7. 6-7.
21. Ibid., 1, 9. 11.
22. Dante, *Convivio,* p. 41.
23. Dante, *De vulg. eloq.,* pp. 88-89.
24. Ibid., pp. 62-63.
25. Dante, *Convivio,* 1, 10. 9.
26. Ibid., 1, 11. 1.
27. Ibid., 1, 3. 5.
28. Dante, *De vulg. eloq.,* 1, 17. 2.
29. Ibid., 1, 18. 1.
30. Ibid., 1, 18. 3.
31. Dante, *Epistulae* 5. 19.
32. Dante, *De vulg. eloq.,* 1, 18. 4.
33. Ibid., 1, 18. 5.
34. Hans von Arnim, ed., *Stoicorum veterum fragmenta,* 4 vols. (Stuttgart: Teubner, 1964), fragment 100v. See in this regard the important sources on allegory in ancient times in Lucius Cornutus, *Theologiae graecae compendium,* ed. Carl Lang (Bibliotheca scriptorum et romanorum Teubneriana, 1881), and Heraclitus (Herclides), *Allegoriae homericae,* ed. Soc. Philolog. (Bonn Sodales, 1910).
35. Origenes, Prin, 2, 2, 4; Isidor of Seville, *Etymologicorum sive originum libri,* bk. 7, chap. 7. Cf. bk. 8, 7, 3.
36. Fabius Fulgentius, *De continentia vergiliana,* ed. Helms (Leipzig, 1898).
37. W. Riedel, ed., *Commentum Bernardus Silvestris super Sex Libros Aeneidos Vergilii* (Greifswald, 1924).
38. Ibid., 1. 10; 3. 8.
39. D. Comparetti, *Virgilio nel Medioevo* (Florence, 1955), p. 137.
40. Seneca *De constitutionibus* 2, 1; Hippolitus Romanus *Refutatio omnium haersum* 5. 25.
41. Salutati, *De laboribus Herculis,* 2 vols., ed. B. L. Ullmann (Zürich: Aedibus Thesauri Mundi, 1951), 1. 5.
42. Ibid., p. 5.
43. Ibid., p. 7.

44. Ibid.

45. Ibid., pp. 7-8.

46. Lactantius, *De divinis institutionibus,* ed. P. L. Migne, 6. 171; Cristoforo Landino, *Reden Cristoforo Landinos,* ed. M. Lentzen (Munich, 1974), p. 22.

47. Ibid.

48. Plato *Phaedrus* 245a; *Ion* 533 e-f; Cicero *Tusculanae* 1, 26. 1; Landino, p. 24.

49. Landino, p. 25.

50. Ibid., pp. 25-26.

51. Aristotle *Topics* 101a 10; 100a 18.

52. Leonardo Bruni, "Ad P. P. Histrum dialogus," in *Prosatori latini del quattrocento,* ed. E. Garin (Milan, 1952), p. 56.

53. Leonardo Bruni, *Humanistische-philosophische Schriften,* Quellen zur Geistesgeschichte des Mittelalters und der Renaissance, Band 1, Veröffentlichungen der Forschungsinstitute an der Universität Leipzig, ed. Hans Baron (Leipzig, Teubner, 1928), p. 89.

54. Leonardo Bruni, *Epistolarum libri,* 8 vols., ed. Lorenzo Mehus (Florence, 1741), 2:108, 126.

55. Bruni, *Schriften,* p. 86.

56. Cicero *Lucullus* 125; *De natura deorum* 2. 58; 4. 417; *De republica* 1. 43; 4. 777.

57. Bruni, *Schriften,* p. 124.

58. Bruni, *Epistolarum,* 1. 19.

59. Angelo Poliziano, *Suetoni expositio,* pp. 435, 499.

60. Poliziano, "Lamia," ed. I. Del Lungo, p. 280; *Praelectio de dialectica,* p. 529.

61. Poliziano, *Oratio super Quintilianus,* ed. Garin, p. 882.

62. Ibid.

63. Ibid. See Ernesto Grassi, *Humanismus und Marxismus* and "Marxism, Humanism, and the Problem of Imagination in Vico's Works," pp. 275-94.

64. G. W. F. Hegel, "Ästhetik," in *Sämtliche Werke,* 12:538.

65. Ibid., p. 535.

66. Cf. Herodotus 1. 64 and Thucydides 1. 134, 4.

67. Aristotle *Poetics* 1459a 4.

68. Ibid., 1457b. Cf. *Rhetoric* 1410b 2; 1459a 5.

69. Aristotle *Poetics* 1459; Aristotle *Rhetoric* 1412a 11.

70. Ibid.

71. Cicero *De oratore* 3. 155-56; 1. 322-23; 3. 155; 1. 323; 3. 156; 1. 323.

72. Ibid., 3. 161; 1. 324.

73. Ibid., 3. 158; 1. 323; 2. 157; 1. 251.

74. See Ernesto Grassi, *Macht des Bildes,* pp. 73 and 169; "Rhetoric and Philosophy," pp. 200-16. Cf. "The Priority of Common Sense and Imagination: Vico's Philosophical Relevance Today," *Social Research* 43 (1976): 533-75.

75. See Pellegrini, Tesauro, and the typical interpretation of Gracián in his theory of *Ingenium* and the witticism.

76. Hugo of St. Victor, *Didascalicon*, 742A 9, 742B 10.

77. Ibid., 742A 5-8.

78. Ibid., 743B 2.

79. Ibid., 743B.

80. Dante, *De vulg. eloq.*, 1, 4. 4.

81. See Ernesto Grassi, "Critical Philosophy or Topical Philosophy? Meditations on the *De nostri temporis studiorum ratione*," in Giorgio Tagliacozzo and Hayden V. White, *Giambattista Vico: An International Symposium* (Baltimore: Johns Hopkins University Press, 1969), pp. 39-50.

Chapter 5

1. P. L. Berger, *Zur Dialektik von Religion und Gesellschaft* (Frankfort/M., 1973), p. 27.

2. Aristotle *De anima* 2. 420b 29.

3. S. Kierkegaard, *Der Begriff Angst* (Hamburg, 1960), pp. 40, 141.

4. Thure von Üxküll, "Semiotik der Angst" (paper read at the symposium, Bad Homburg, December 1977).

5. René Thom, "De l'icone au symbole," in *Modèles mathématiques de la morphogenèse* (Paris, 1974), pp. 247-48.

6. Ibid., pp. 248, 250.

7. S. Freud, *Das Unheimliche* (1919), Studienausgabe (Frankfort/M., 1970), pp. 271, 268, 263.

8. E. Swedenborg, *Himmliche Geheimnisse* (London, 1758), no. 2249, 7014, 1873, 9357.

9. S. Kierkegaard, *Lo specchio della parola*, a cura di E. Valenziani e C. Fabro (Florence, 1948).

10. Ibid., p. 65.

11. Ibid.

12. Ibid., pp. 71, 63.

13. Ibid., pp. 68, 75.

14. Ibid., p. 81.

15. Dante, *De vulg. eloq.*, 1, 4. 4.

16. C. Baudelaire, *Correspondances, Oeuvres complètes* (Paris, 1954), p. 87.